EVERYTHING
I Know About Life
I Learned From
MY HORSE

Gwen Petersen

Voyageur Press

First published in 2009 by Voyageur Press, an imprint of MBI Publishing Company, 400 First Avenue North, Suite 300, Minneapolis, MN 55401 USA

The information in this book is true and complete to the best of our knowledge. All recommendations are made without any guarantee on the part of the author or Publisher, who also disclaims any liability incurred in connection with the use of this data or specific details.

We recognize, further, that some words, model names, and designations mentioned herein are the property of the trademark holder. We use them for identification purposes only. This is not an official publication.

Voyageur Press titles are also available at discounts in bulk quantity for industrial or sales-promotional use. For details write to Special Sales Manager at MBI Publishing Company, 400 First Avenue North, Suite 300, Minneapolis, MN 55401 USA.

To find out more about our books, visit us online at www.voyageurpress.com.

ISBN-13: 978-0-7603-3690-8

Editor: Margret Aldrich
Designer: Sara Holle
Cover Designer: Wendy Lutge

Printed in United States of America

Image credits

Voyageur Press Archive: 5, 17, 65, 69, 91, 101, 133, 139, 157, 163, 220, 223

Getty Images/Hulton Archive: 14 (Lambert), 18 (Fox), 54 (Three Lions), 208 (FPG).

Library of Congress: 23, 31, 37, 40, 43, 47, 52–53, 59, 61, 70, 75, 84, 94–95, 100, 115, 116, 125, 128–129, 146, 148, 154, 165, 174, 176, 198, 207, 212–213

Bill Manns/The Art Archive: 86, 122–123

Underwood Photo Archives/SuperStock: Front cover, 186

Library of Congress Cataloging-in-Publication Data

Petersen, Gwen.
  Everything I know about life I learned from my horse / Gwen Petersen.
     p. cm.
  ISBN 978-0-7603-3690-8 (hb w/ jkt)
  1. Horsemanship—Anecdotes. 2. Horses—Anecdotes. 3. Petersen, Gwen. 4. Human-animal relationships—Anecdotes. I. Title.
  SF309.P48 2009
  636.1—dc22

                         2009004519

Dedication
To my horses, of course.

Contents

Be advised that loving horses is a surefire way to let the world know you're slightly bonkers. Once hooked on horses, you'll give your beloved steeds more love and attention than you do your spouse, children, or parents. Dating couples have been known to go separate ways when he or she prefers four-footed equines to a hot date.

Horsing Around One
Wherein you learn that you know more about moon travel than you know about purchasing a horse. And wherein you learn that you should take horse-trader stories seriously.

Horsing Around Two
Rules of Horsemanship:
Wherein you learn about Out West hayburners, and wherein you also learn what "saddle sore" means.

Horsing Around Three
Wherein you learn that some horses are better babysitters than television, ice cream, or a pet baboon.

Part Four PRANCING AND DANCING 71

Everybody loves a parade, so they say. You and your horse do too. Dressed in your spiffiest riding duds, a smile pasted on your face, you lift a hand and wave graciously to the watching crowd.

Everybody loves the stories of the West. Which may be why dude (guest) ranches are so popular. Sometimes gal guests sign on hoping to find a willing cowboy. (Generally speaking, cowboys are more than willing to . . . no, let's not go there.) Often guy guests like to stomp around in cowboy boots à la John Wayne.

Horsing Around Fourteen
Wherein you learn how to wrangle dudes and never lose your smile.

Horsing Around Fifteen
Wherein you learn that Scotch is bubbly and how to name a horse.

Horsing Around Sixteen
Wherein you learn that sometimes a good horse is the answer to an irritating problem. And wherein you learn a song to keep in your heart.

Horsing Around Seventeen
Wherein you learn what it means to do a wrangler's job.

Horsing Around Eighteen
Wherein you learn that all sorts of folk want to "help" at a branding.

There is no end, no bottom, no final story if you're a horse lover. Some stories are humorous, some are nostalgic, and many can be tragic. Life with your horse (or mule if you're into extralong ears) is a blessing for which you can't give enough thanks.

Preface

In the "old days," way before digital anything, traveling photographers would trek through neighborhoods leading a pony or two. These wee steeds most often bore pinto markings, possibly because spackle patterns showed up better in black-and-white photos. Your parents hurried[1] to have you, their li'l darling, photographed astride Li'l Dobbin. You can still remember petting the silky, curling mane. You loved that half-pint cayuse. You wanted the pony man to adopt you. Or leave a pony in your yard.

Your parents did their best to raise a normal kid. They provided food, shelter, and education. They let you have pet dogs and cats. They even let you raise baby chicks to chickenhood, but they claimed a backyard in a city was inadequate for keeping a horse, even a little one. Your passion did not wane. At Saturday matinees where the local theater showed kid-flicks, you fell in undying love with Silver, the Lone Ranger's gleaming white stallion.[2] And when Tonto, the L. R.'s faithful sidekick, galloped his paint horse, Scout, into the sunset, you got chills.[3] Watching Roy Rogers and Trigger, Dale Evans and Buttercup prance across the movie screen

---

1 Mom and Dad "hurried" because the tantrum you threw had your face turning blue.
2 You practiced "Hi-Yo Silverrr" way more than your piano lessons.
3 You also practiced "Git 'em up, Scout" with irritating frequency.

caused heart palpitations. And they could sing, too. (Dale and Roy, not Trigger and Buttercup).[4]

Add to those influences the summers you spent at your grandparents' farm where you were allowed to ride one of Granddad's racing pacers. Seated high up on a sixteen-hands pacing horse made you Queen of the Universe. You began collecting horse books, horse statuettes, horse trinkets, horse blankets.

And then you moved Out West and found yourself in Horse Heaven. You are irreversibly afflicted with a love for horses, or maybe you're terminally insane. Don't worry about it. The rest of the world is merely envious.

Whatever your reasons, grab your hat, saddle up, and let's ride.

---

4 Actually, Trigger and Buttercup did the prancing. Roy and Dale just sat there—singing.

Part One

HOOKED ON HAYBURNERS

Be advised that loving horses is a surefire way to let the world know you're slightly bonkers. Once hooked on horses, you'll give your beloved steeds more love and attention than you do your spouse, children, or parents. Dating couples have been known to go separate ways when he or she prefers four-footed equines to a hot date.

ACQUIRING A STEED

*Wherein you learn that you know more about moon
travel than you know about purchasing a horse. And wherein
you learn that you should take horse-trader stories seriously.*

'Tis on a nice morning when you ride into town (on a train).
There you are—Out West and horseless. To remedy that
wretched condition, you set about finding and buying the perfect steed. When you see the ad, "For sale: Fifteen-year-old
Quarter horse," you hurry to dial the number, breathlessly
take down directions, and speed thither, horse trailer in
tow.

In a small round corral, there he stands, a medium-tall
pinto pony with nice conformation, if a bit chunky. The
owner has him saddled and demonstrates by riding him
around the corral at a walk, trot, and lope. Then you step
up into the saddle. The horse behaves wonderfully. You
are thrilled, excited, ecstatic. You practically drool as you
fork over the cash and become a horse owner. The trader
unsaddles, halters this unbelievably marvelous, incredibly
gorgeous steed, leads him into your trailer, and ties him to
a rail.

"I'll just give you the halter," says the trader, a raspy-voiced old cowboy with a gray mustache and a twinkle in the eye.[5]

You depart, proud new owner of Patches—a brown and white pinto pony, yours to own and love.

When you turn him out, you feed him some grain just to let him know he has a good home. Next day you take a halter and a bucket of oats, intending to catch and ride your new steed. You shake the grain bucket. Patches edges close. Another shake. Patches dips his nose in the bucket and slurps. You attempt to ease the halter onto his head. Patches ducks. For the next hour you do your best, but that blasted horse will *not* be caught. Finally, you haze him into a corner near a gate leading into a small pen. First you open the gate, then you drop a trail of oats from open gate to mid-pen where you pour out a heaping pile.[6] Once he spots the grain, he starts lapping up the kernels and follows the goodies into the pen. With a soaring Wonder Woman leap, you close the gate behind him. "Aha!" you screech. Patches only looks at you from big, brown, innocent eyes and allows you to halter him as if to say, "What's all the fuss?" That horse *always* has to be tricked in order to be caught.

He has another bad habit. Twice, good ol' Patches unloads you from his back, usually after he's settled down and seems to be behaving. Once he's dumped you, he never waits around. He just snorts a snotty snort, kicks up his heels, and takes off. After which, you institute a sore-footed hike back to the home pasture to find Patches waiting to be let in. Oh, yes. *Now* he lets you catch him.

Research on Patches' early history turns up a surprise. It seems this particular equine was once one of a bucking string for a rodeo company. Then apparently he grew bored with bucking, so they used him for ordinary ranch work.

5 Do not put faith in any old-cowboy horse trader who has a twinkle—and they all do.
6 Oats to a horse are the ice-cream sundaes of their world.

He developed into a pretty good cow horse—except for the times he'd recall his bucking-horse youth and dump his rider.

You aren't made of rubber and you are also chicken.[7] When along comes a young cowboy looking to purchase a horse, it doesn't take more than a hot minute to let him coax you into selling Patches. The cowpony and the cowboy get along beautifully. Cowboy is a good roper. If Patches resists being caught, Cowboy merely shakes out a loop and Patches stands stock still. He does *not* like being roped. He even quits his reminiscing-type bucking habit, mainly because the young cowpoke can ride anything with hair and four legs. Patches never throws Cowboy even once. Patches, figuring that's no fun, quits trying.

You wish you'd known about the rope trick when you'd owned that sorry horse. You couldn't and can't rope for sour owls, but you're sure you could've shook a loop.

7   You still are.

Horsing Around

2

RULES OF HORSEMANSHIP
#1: GET MOUNTED #2: STAY MOUNTED

*Wherein you learn about Out West hayburners, and
wherein you also learn what "saddle sore" means.*

You launch your early Out West horse know-how by helping "take a string of horses" to a far pasture. Any outdoor
activity Out West means starting the day before sunup.[8]
You stagger to the corral in the dark and lean over the top
rail. Your two fellow *experienced* riders assign you a steed
they claim is "gentle as a lamb" and "absolutely reliable"
but has a gait that's "maybe a little rough." They assure
you that your four-footed hayburner has "never bucked
yet."[9] Your gentle-as-a-lamb charger is a dingy, tattle-tale
gray with mane and tail hanging in burr-choked clumps.
He's a sort of off-white Lone Ranger reject and has reached
an age qualifying him to be in the Book of Records. His
name is Buckie.

---

8   Western myth claims that one must rise and be ready to ride before sunup. Don't
    mess with myths.
9   You wonder if that means the beast is biding his time.

Before your adventure can begin, you must saddle old Buckie. Differences in saddles abound, depending on where you live on the planet. The standard American western cowboy saddle can be a character-building test of fortitude, attitude, and survival skill. The western saddle is not a graceful postage-stamp bit of upholstered leather upon which the posterior reposes gracefully. No, it's a deep, leather, chairlike, soft-as-a-rock contraption upon which the posterior can bounce like a disorganized jumping bean. Stirrups the size of shoe boxes dangle from each side of said saddle.

Without previous weightlifting experience, the average beginning rider will find the average western saddle as easy to pick up as trying to bench-press a freight train. The true-blue born-in-the-saddle *western* horseman or horsewoman, no matter how scrawny, can one-handedly sling a saddle aboard any size equine. This accounts for the prevalence of shoulder-socket bursitis, slipped discs, and ruptured rotator cuffs among horse enthusiasts.

Start with the saddle blanket.[10] Smooth the blanket evenly from withers toward tail. Next, approach the ton of leather saddle. Flip the near stirrup over the saddle horn, grasp the pommel, and hoist. Imagine you're an Olympic shot-putter. Bend the knees, lift at the same time, and toss the outfit atop ol' Buckie's back[11] aiming to center the front end (where the horn rises) above his withers. Your dictionary might tell you that "wither" means to wilt, dry up, or shrivel. "Withers" plural, however, is that area atop the shoulders on a horse. It's the north end of the spinal column just behind the mane. Some horses have sky-reaching, saddle-splitting withers so high and sharp you can almost see the vertebrae poking

10 Saddle blankets come in interesting patterns, and make attractive small rugs for hallways, wall hangings, and gifts to greenhorns.
11 Be grateful Buckie is a *short* horse.

through the hide. Ol' Buckie has mutton-shoulder withers, which is to say his spinal ridge is shaped like a marshmallow. [12]

Watch out for over-enthusiasm when slinging the saddle. It could arc high and crash to earth on the other side of old Buckie. On the other hand, if your toss is short, you might slam Buckie's side. He doesn't care, but some horses might object. Buckie, having reached his golden years, no longer worries. He spraddles his feet, grips the ground, and hunches up for the next assault.

Next task: Bridling ol' Buckie. Grasp the bridle[13] and attempt to slip it onto Buckie's head. He will either a) throw his head up out of reach, or b) refuse to unclench his teeth, or c) jerk his head away when you try to fit the poll strap over his ears, or d) all of the above.

At long last, saddling and bridling having been accomplished in proper sequence, the moment has arrived to *get on*. That's when you realize that Buckie might be a short horse, but he's still taller than you are. The stirrup hangs there, offering you a challenge. If you've been working out, if you're as robust and fit as a track and field star, if you're a gymnast, then mounting will be a snap.[14] Gather Buckie's reins, place your left foot in the near stirrup,[15] and swing lithely aboard in one smooth motion. That's what *should* happen. There's an excellent chance your ascent is more apt to resemble a crab crawling up the side of a cliff.

To retain your dignity (if that's important), lead Buckie alongside a rail fence, a car bumper, a large boulder, or into a

---

12 If he's round-shouldered, the saddle has a tendency to slide sideways or forward, especially when traveling down a steep hillside. You could find yourself astride the horse's neck.
13 A contraption of straps with a metal crosspiece called a "bit" that goes in the horse's mouth.
14 You, however, are going to have to struggle mightily.
15 You know it's the "near" side when your left hand points toward the horse's head and the right hand can point to the steed's aft region.

deep ditch. This puts your feet on a level, more or less, with the stirrup. Step aboard. Once in the saddle, assume control of the reins. Buckie's docile, but he's a glutton. He constantly lowers his head to grab a grass blade, a weed, a thistle top. Each time he lunges, the action jerks on the reins, which you're holding. Your arm is yanked forward. It's a little like the start of being drawn and quartered.

Remember, you're "taking a string of horses to pasture." The "string" numbers five head. Your two friends each lead a pair, leaving you in charge of one cayuse—a tall, black-and-white paint. You grasp the lead rope of the paint. The group moves out. Well, your two partners on their horses move out. Buckie proves he's never been on a racing circuit. For the entire trip, you ride drag.[16] During a cattle drive, smaller calves and slow cows that can't keep up drag along behind the main bunch. The last drover "brings up the drag" or "rides drag." This position is usually assigned to the very young, the crippled, the decrepit, or the greenhorn. Pick your preferred category.

Don't be depressed. Riding drag is the perfect location from which to contemplate the fairy-tale blue of the western sky as your trusty mustang carries you fearlessly forward across brush-covered rangeland. Take pleasure in watching sagehens—spooked by the horses—take flight and skitter from bush to bush. Enjoy the feel of the sun warm on your back as Buckie's head bobs before you, his tacky mane flopping rhythmically. Keep your eyes gimleted so you can search the horizons for the occasional outlaw, or roving band of hostiles, or possibly a Handsome Stranger on a white stallion. Enjoy the way your body balances, lissome as a dancer's, at one with your steed's strides while the breeze slips caressing fingers through your tawny hair.[17] You might even warble a

16 This has nothing to do with kinky dress behavior.
17 Never mind whether or not you *have* tawny-type hair. Out West, every woman's crowning glory automatically turns tawny once she climbs on a horse.

chorus of *I've Got Spurs That Jingle, Jangle, Jingle.*

This rich fantasy life may last as long as twenty or thirty minutes, depending on your personal fitness. Then reality strikes in the form of painful twinges. Your body stops being lissome. The earlier description of Buckie's gait as "a little rough" fell short of total accuracy. Your bones develop more jangles than the song. In addition, the big black and white paint steed you are leading has decided not to wait for you and Buckie. He gallops ahead, hits the end of the halter rope, and the jolt nearly flips you out of the saddle. The paint then decides to change tactics. He follows along meek as a mouse for perhaps six steps, then stops dead in his tracks, which almost yanks you backward out of the saddle. To prevent another drawing and quartering experience, dally the lead rope around the saddle horn.[18]

Try meditating the pain away. Forget that your shoulders hurt, your knees throb, rope burns sting your palms, and you feel sure you have blisters on your posterior. Your body ping-pongs on a saddle big enough to accommodate the singing fat lady of the opera. You attempt to maintain a grip on Buckie's chubby sides, which is like trying to clasp a wine barrel with chopsticks. As excruciating pain knifes through your knee joints and your flopping form further destabilizes, you may be tempted to clutch the saddle horn.[19]

Soldier on. What else can you do? Your two host riders are way up ahead. They're riding side by side, chatting and laughing, [20] each easily leading a pair of extra mounts.

As the eons roll by, your stomach says you haven't eaten since last year. At about the time you have given up hope of living to see another dawn, a halt is called to rest the *horses.* A creek gurgles nearby. You realize your thirst is nearly equal

18 Be wary. Take care the rope doesn't saw a gash in your leg next time the horse jerks back.

19 Shame on you. A true Westerner would fall to his/her death before clutching.

20 You harbor hateful feelings toward them—the humans, not the horses.

to your leg pains. Gather together the various parts of your body and prepare to dismount. Your goal: to draw your off leg up and over Buckie's rump and then carefully lower yourself earthward. You discover you've lost all control. Your form drops like a sack of compost. Thudding to the ground, your legs fail entirely and your torso telescopes into your boots.[21] Crawl to the creek edge, slake your thirst, and then locomote to the shade of the nearest tree. Inspect the insides of your knees. Ground hamburger surrounded by fat, watery blisters has replaced skin. Your spine feels as if spikes have been driven between each vertebra. You now know why those pioneer women *walked* alongside the wagons.

Fortunately, the smashed peanut butter and jelly sandwich you are told is lunch puts a weensy bit of life back into your body. Very weensy. It's time to face the grisly prospect of once again mounting up. You stifle moans of terminal pain and haul your tortured torso into the saddle.

As the ordeal recommences, ease pressure on throbbing joints and blistered knees by dangling your feet out of the stirrups. Accept shame and cling to the saddle horn while your abused body bops around like a rubber ball tied to a paddle. Buckie, plodding along on four flat tires and a broken axle, will pay no mind to your riding technique. As you attempt to blot out the agony, hallucinations come and go.

After many days of healing up, you begin to feel pride in having helped "take a string of horses to pasture." You also learn that Buckie is a local legend as the roughest-gaited horse in the country. For awhile you're a tad piqued at your new western friends. Then one day a visitor from New York pleads to "go on a horseback ride." You offer her the chance to ride a gentle horse by the name of Buckie. Assure the visitor that you yourself rode old Buckie and he never bucked once.

21 Save face by pretending you're joking.

Horsing Around

KID HORSES

*Wherein you learn that some horses are better babysitters
than television, ice cream, or a pet baboon.*

You acquire Pistachio from a retiring sheepherder who wants
his mount to "go to a good home." Pistachio is about a hundred
in horse years. Grayish white, he is spackled with dark spots
of no particular design. He owns a pair of huge, dark eyes that
seem to say he holds untold wisdom deep within. Maybe he
does. He never speaks of it, though he does have a habit of
snuffling a lot. You can discuss any subject with Pistachio and
receive snuffling commentaries in return.

On the afternoon you take a friend and her three-year-
old toddler out to the pasture, Pistachio proves his worth.
You and said friend feed P. a few carrots. Toddler does
too.[22] P. politely consumes all. The day is clear and sunny;
the sky is a forever dome of blue; a pair of eagles dive and
skim toward the ground, searching for a gopher or rabbit
lunch. While you and friend raptly watch the aerial show,
Toddler takes it upon herself to tend to Pistachio. When

22   Toddler shortens Pistachio's name to "Pissy."

you and Mom turn around, there stands Toddler—between the horse's front legs. Pistachio moves nary a muscle. The child trots in a figure eight between his legs and scoots under his belly. Pistachio doesn't move.

For long moments you and Toddler's Mama freeze. You don't want to yell and scare Toddler or Pistachio. Finally, the kidlet emerges from beneath the horse's belly and cruises round to stand facing him, looking up. Pistachio lowers his big head and snuffles her hair. Toddler laughs, turns, and runs to her mother. "Horsey, horsey," says Toddler. Mother scoops up the child. Both you and Toddler's Mom let out held-in breaths. Pistachio finally moves, moseys over, and snuffles Toddler again, this time held firmly in Mama's arms.

Pistachio earns a good home for his remaining years. You generously give him to Toddler's parents to the delight of Toddler—and Pistachio. He likes to nap on warm afternoons. A time or two, Toddler joins him. To see a horse lying down stretched out on its side and a child snuggled up against its belly—both snoozing—makes a fantastic Christmas card.

Horsing Around

COPING WITH PRO-TEM EQUINES AND ODDBALL HORSES

Wherein you become a short-term owner of a variety of steeds. And wherein you learn that some horses have BBs for brains.

Lonesome

"He's an orphan colt," says your friend, Sandy. "His mama died. The owner has been bottle-feeding him. Owner wants to find a good home for the colt."

That's how you acquire a cute horse colt, coppery red in color except for an anklet of white on a hind leg. You name him Lonesome because he seems a little sad when he first arrives. Or maybe you think he *should* be sad, having lost his mama.

Lonesome settles in with your other steeds.[23] Counting Lonesome, you are indentured in the service of six equines—one saddle mare, Becky; a miniature mare, Pretty Girl, with foal at her side, Cinnamon; and a miniature gelding, Cherokee.[24]

---

23   Yes, other steeds. Like most horse enthusiasts, you've somehow acquired multiple equines. You now know what the term "horse poor" means.
24   See Horsing Around Twenty-Seven for full miniature-horse disclosure.

As a yearling, Lonesome's stature predicted he'd remain a short horse. Apparently your pasture grass is extremely nutritious, because Lonesome grows and then grows some more. You start calling him Big Red. He starts calling himself King of the Range. Because he'd been a pet and hand-fed on bottled milk, his attitude is that all people-creatures are born to serve. He considers the miniature horses toys he should chase, so he does. But the minis, though small, can dodge and duck back. By the time Red cranks his big body around to pursue a back-tracking mini, the little one has zipped behind the horse trailer.

Big Red especially enjoys tormenting Cinnamon, the miniature filly. Her Mama, Pretty Girl, tries to protect Cinnamon by letting fly with both hind heels. Unfortunately, the blows merely land on Big Red's chest, having about as much effect as tossing pebbles at a tank. But Cinnamon has more than one protector. When she grows tired of being chased, she darts up to Becky, the saddle mare. Big Red might think he's King, but Becky *knows* she is Queen. All she has to do is give Red a "look," and he immediately loses interest in chasing.

Big Red's curiosity nearly kills him. One morning he sees something wiggling—and coiling up. Aha, something else to pursue! He nuzzles the critter. In a blink two fangs strike him in the nose.

Though you didn't see the actual exchange, you are appalled to discover poor Red, his nose grossly swollen. The veterinarian arrives. Big Red is loaded into the horse trailer and taken to the clinic. It's touch and go, but two weeks and several hundred dollars later, Red comes home. Never again does he try to kiss a snake.

A sociable horse, Big Red enjoys visiting neighbors. A retired couple live in a dwelling on some property adjacent to your north pasture. There's a gate between your land and the drive into their place, but occasionally the neighbors forget to close it. Red, however, has learned to check regularly. An open gate to Big Red is an invitation to call. Time of day—or night—makes no difference.[25] One nighttime visit nearly gives the neighbor lady a heart attack.

At three a.m., she hears someone knocking. At first she thinks a tree branch has fallen on the roof, then realizes, duh, the house sits on a patch of treeless prairie. The knocking persists. Clad in her chenille robe and fluffy slippers, Neighbor Lady opens the door and finds herself lip to lip with Big Red. He smiles and attempts to enter.

"Shoo," says Neighbor Lady. "Shoo! Shoo!"

When daylight arrives, you respond to Neighbor Lady's phone call and trek over to retrieve your wandering horse. It turns out that Red had climbed the five steps to the porch so he could slurp all the sunflower seeds from Neighbor Lady's bird feeder. Maybe he knocked at her door to beg for more?

Big Red's social calls extend farther than the close neighbor. On a particular afternoon, he jumps the cattle guard separating his pasture from the county road and off he goes. Two miles along, he stops to talk with some horses he spots in a field next to a ranch house. Apparently happy to have found new friends, Red strolls into the ranch yard.

You receive another phone call and make yet another horse retrieval.

By the time he's four, Red is halter broke, trailer broke, hoof-trimming broke, and driving you crazy. He needs work. He's big and strong and always looking for something to do. He doesn't have any buck in him, but he's green and you don't have enough expertise to turn him into a respectable cow horse. You take him to a local horse trainer[26] and lo and behold, Big Red turns out to have a natural slow-gait. It's like riding a rocking chair and he never seems to tire.

25 As mentioned, he is a *sociable* horse.
26 You will spend a potload of money on horse training.

35

You call your friend, Sandy, from whom you originally obtained Lonesome, aka Big Red. Sandy and Scott Sallee, operators of Blackmountain Outfitters, are often seeking horses—hardy enough to use in the mountains during hunting season and gentle enough to carry dudes in the summer camping season.

For the three years of his company, Big Red has cost you five times more than his sale price, made you better acquainted with neighbors, and messed with your mind.

Joker

The horse ranch—facetiously dubbed the Flaming Flamingo Ranch[27]—sells you a cute, coal-black three-year-old. His heritage is of the unknown variety, but his conformation is excellent and he can prance like a Disney animation. You name him Joker because he smiles a lot. Horses don't smile? This one does. Followed by a fit of pitching. Still, Joker behaves like a kitten when you want to catch and saddle him and for twenty minutes or so allows you to enjoy a pleasant ride.

You're not sure what is wrong with Joker. After the umpteenth time he tosses a fit (sometimes you stay on, sometimes not), you sell him to your sister for a dollar. She is a much better horsewoman than you, but even she finds out that Joker can't be trusted. Like people critters, horse critters come in an infinite range of sizes, conformations, colors, attitudes, temperaments, and styles.

Canner prices at the auction yard bring enough to buy dinner at the Stockman Café.

27 The ranch owner's wife collects flamingo art, flamingo ceramics, and flamingo doodads. Her manicured front lawn boasts a dozen yard-tall flaming pink flamingo replicas.

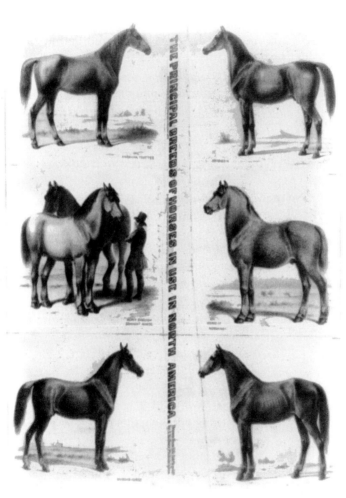

THE PRINCIPAL BREEDS OF HORSES IN USE IN NORTH AMERICA.

The Gift Horse

"No, thank you," you say, "don't need another horsie,
I've way too many, now don't try to force me!"

"But he's a baby, just nine months old,
Raised on a bottle, a poor orphan colt.

"Dog gentle and loving, you really should
Give him a home, he's so sweet and good."

"No thank you," you say, "I've plenty of steeds,
More than enough to meet my needs."

"But this one is small, he won't grow too big,
If you can't ride him, he'll pull a rig.

"He's red all over like a robin's breast,
With one white foot, you know he's the best.

"I'll let you have him for a paltry song,
I'll even deliver, it won't take long."

So, now you own a little red horse,
Cute as a button, you love him of course.

He's a sweet little stud, he comes when you call,
He loves everybody, he's no trouble at all.

But your mare, she hates him, she whips him bad,
She bites, she kicks, she's doggone mad.

Her attitude's nasty; she's plumb incensed,
She spooks Little Red through the west side fence.

Which broke three wires and left a big hole—
In the fence, not the horse—he just rolled.

Now you've a fence that needs repair,
To the tune of dollars that you can't spare.

And you must close off a separate pasture,
You'll need money to pay for this disaster.

And come next Tuesday, the vet will arrive
To change the mindset of the little red guy.

For your gift horse, you've lots of expense,
Sometimes free makes no darned sense.

If you want some advice, when someone asks
To give you a colt, no strings attached—

Run for the hills, lock all your doors!
Don't answer the phone, begging ignore!

Heed this advice or one day you'll own
A little red colt—and a *big bank loan*.

Part Two

RIDIN', RIDIN', RIDIN'

Once you've found and purchased the mount you know you'll love forever, you'll spend great wads of time, money, and effort on riding anywhere, anytime, for any reason.

BUYING THE HORSE OF YOUR DREAMS

Wherein you ride up a cloudy draw in pursuit of your dream horse—Smokey, a prince among horses.

The day your local veterinarian invites you to ride along to a horse ranch turns out to be an auspicious occasion. That's when you meet Smokey. The rancher and the vet hunker down near a set of corrals and settle in for a long gab session. The rancher tells you—casually—to go "bring in the bunch."

"Take Banjo, there," says Mr. Rancher. "He's a stallion, but he's gentle."

You say nary a word. You can't. Your mouth has gone dry.[1] A stallion?[2]

"Just follow that draw and you'll see 'em," is your only instruction. You climb aboard Banjo and with a great deal of assumed nonchalance,[3] you ride away . . . and away . . . and away. Turns out the "bunch" is grazing in a high pasture up in the hills.

---

1 Leg pulling is an art form Out West. If a rise can be elicited, you can count on the story being repeated unto perpetuity.
2 Where's the Lone Ranger when you need him?
3 Always keep a quart of assumed nonchalance handy.

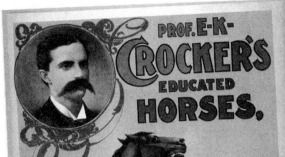

PROF. E-K- CROCKER'S EDUCATED HORSES.

THE GREATEST BARREL ACT EVER SEEN

PONIES, DONKEYS & MULES.

Fortunately, Banjo seems to know where he is going, so you let him—but you hold him to a walk. With your history of airborne departure from a saddle, you don't want to tempt fate.

The horse bunch, when you finally spot them, makes a scene that would cause Robert Redford to whisper his throat raw. In a small meadow as green as an Irish shamrock, a dozen horses graze. Sunlight shines on them as if the Deity has arranged a special backlight. A fringe of pine trees and aspens frame the glade.[4]

In silence, you guide Banjo around the perimeter of the meadow till you are above the horses and gently begin urging them downhill. Thankfully, they, like Banjo, know what to do and start moseying along. You let them mosey. No yee-haw rousting.[5] As the ranch buildings come into view, "the bunch" begins to pick up speed, breaks into a mild gallop, and swarms through the open gate of the corral where the rancher had placed some piles of hay.[6]

By now you're on the gallop too. You pull up just in time to leap off and shut the corral gate moments ahead of Mr. Rancher and Mr. Veterinarian. Remember your assumed nonchalance? Deepen it. And savor the look of restrained surprise on Mr. R's and Mr. V's faces.[7]

The horses munch on the hay piles. One small licorice-colored horse with dark gray dapples looks up and stares. Right at you. Mr. Rancher indicates a tall sorrel.

"That sorrel there oughta suit you," he drawls.

"I like that little smoke-colored one," you reply.

And shortly you become the new owner of Smokey, a horse you still treasure in your heart.

4 There are few sights grander or more guaranteed to bring a lump to your throat than a picturesque landscape featuring horses.
5 Recall your history. No yee-hawing!
6 Bribery is *always* a useful tool when dealing with horses.
7 But in your head, shout, "Hah!"

HORSEBACK GAMES

Wherein you learn how to whoop it up in gymkhanas. And wherein Smokey is a steed with attitude and pizzazz.

Smokey loves gymkhanas.[8] Half Welsh pony and half Morgan horse, Smokey can outrun a thoroughbred—at least for a short distance. He's only fourteen hands, but put him in a race and he digs in, his legs flashing like hairy eggbeaters.

You are pretty smug the day you ride as one of a three-person team in a relay race at the local fairgrounds. Six trios have entered the contest. Of the six, you and your two pals, Gloria and Leslie, represent the only female riders—well, except for Ericka Knutson, a tall, long-legged blonde astride a matching tall, long-legged blonde Palomino. Ericka is part of one of the men's groups. She looks like a Viking princess and she can ride, oh my.[9] On that Palomino she's taken prizes in barrel racing.

The teams compete against the clock; each team member gallops around the track and passes the baton to the next

8 Gymkhanas: Games and novelty events on horseback—sometimes more novel than you wanted.
9 She can't help it if boys, men, and codgers ogle her, run into walls, and drool when they are in her vicinity.

rider. Dropping the baton disqualifies a team. Drawn straws put Ericka and her crew (also mounted on leggy steeds) just ahead of your bunch (the very last to go, with you as the third rider).[10]

Ericka is the other team's third rider and when she grabs the baton and takes off, all you can see is a streak of yellow, a regular comet's tail of golden horse and golden girl zooming around the track. You're not surprised when Ericka's team makes the best time—so far. The watching crowd cheers the Viking princess.

You, Gloria, and Leslie are up next—and you are the last rider.

You and Smokey are edgy. Gloria makes the first lap. She's mounted on Bacon, a sturdy bay who circles the oval track in commendable speed. Then Leslie's up on Cherrypicker, a shiny red sorrel. She takes the baton on the fly and streaks around the track like a speeding bullet.

You step up to the plate or, in this case, to the starting line. Smokey dances, wanting to go. You turn him in a circle and back to the line. Here comes your teammate. Leaning from the saddle, she holds out the baton while still at a dead run. Leaning over Smokey's neck, you thunder alongside and grab onto the baton. Then you turn Smokey loose.

You can hear shouts from the crowd. On the far side of the track, there's a gate. Somebody has opened it. As you pound into the curve, Smokey shoots straight on through the gate. You rein him around in a big circle and thunder back onto the track. You're not going to quit. You whomp Smokey on his rear with the baton. His ears flick; he practically takes wing. You cross the finish line at jet speed. And you lose the race by four seconds.

Miss Viking princess claims her prize, then comes over to where you, Smokey, your teammates, and their horses are lingering like dropped laundry.

10   At drawing straws, you're pathetic.

"You know," says Ericka, "you really should have won." She pats Smokey's sweaty neck. "This little guy sure can run."

"Thanks," you say, feeling a whole lot better. And you also find yourself truly liking the Viking princess.

RODEO AND OTHER WAYS TO HURT YOURSELF

*Wherein you learn to ride a shovel, and that it's best
to keep a goodly supply of Band-Aids near.*

In the field just beyond the south end of the county fairgrounds arena, your family's workhorse, Doodle, munches grass. You stand next to him, looping a garland of petunias over the brass knobs of Doodle's polished horse collar.

You are in charge of this afternoon's Parent and Kid Scoop Shovel race, always a crowd pleaser. One person, usually the father, rides a horse, while another person, usually the kid, rides a scoop shovel pulled behind the horse.[11] The winner receives a prize; this year it's a pair of black and tan cowboy boots with yellow and red dragons inset on fourteen-inch tops. Your eldest son[12] has his heart set on winning those dragon boots. He's dashing toward you now, his eyes the size of ping-pong balls.

---

11 You don't need skill for this event, or brains.
12 Or daughter or niece or nephew or a random passing youngster if you're not married or without a suitable kid.

"Mom! Mom! Dad can't ride! He sprained his ankle in the calf-roping!"

"Oh, m'gosh. . . ."

Your offspring interrupts your attempt to be a concerned wife. "He's okay, he's okay. They took him to town to the clinic to make sure his leg isn't broke, but he won't get back in time to ride Doodle![13] You'll have to do it!"

"I'm not your father," you point out.

"That's okay. Rules just say parent and child—doesn't *have* to be a dad."[14]

Saddles are not allowed in the shovel race. Visualizing yourself trying to ride bareback aboard barrel-shaped Doodle gives you a lot of pause.[15]

As gently as possible you tell your offspring that if you fall off, you'll both be disqualified.

"No problem," says the child of your loins,[16] "I'll ride Doodle. You ride the shovel."

You argue that you have never ridden a shovel and don't plan on doing so now. The counterargument is that all you have to do is sit on the scoop and hang onto the handle while your son, on Doodle, gallops the perimeter of the arena. (You don't *really* believe he's trying to kill you.[17])

The winner of the argument dashes off to inform the judges of the change while you lead Doodle the length of the arena to join the other shovel-race participants. Your son is standing next to his father, freshly returned from the clinic, where, presumably, all his parts were declared serviceable. Your dearly beloved, the man you promised to cleave to 'til death—possibly this very day—wears a sheepish grin and

---

13 A twelve-year-old has no sympathy genes.
14 A twelve-year-old has unassailable logic.
15 As well as heart palpitations.
16 Why is loins a plural word? Do people have more than one loin per body?
17 On the other hand . . .

a pair of crutches. He gimps up to Doodle and begins making harness adjustments.

Doodle's paprika-colored hide glistens; the petunia posies on his collar bob merrily. A yard-and-a-half behind him, the aluminum scoop shovel—your future chariot—gleams like that proverbial silver lining under that proverbial cloud. The shovel handle points toward Doodle's tail. A singletree is anchored crosswise at the base of the shovel. Leather tug lines lead from the singletree, loop through the shovel handle, cross over Doodle's rump, and fasten to rings on his posie-bedecked collar.

You study the contraption. Gloom descends. Your stomach does a few somersaults. Your ever-concerned spouse, the man you suspect deliberately sprained his ankle, presses a pair of leather gloves on you, claiming they will keep your hands from blistering. Blistering?

Gingerly, you lower your posterior, frog-bend your legs, brace your feet on the crosspiece, double your torso forward, and grip the shovel handle. The view before you is not that inspiring, nor can the chimp-in-a-tree posture be termed dignified. You note a suspicious twitch wrinkle the corners of a certain crutch-user's mouth. If you live, you may have to kill him.

Your son leaps aboard Doodle and states he'll take a practice turn so's you'll get the feel of "shovelin'." He guides Doodle sedately in a large circle. The scoop glides over the graded soft turf. Your spirits lift. This isn't bad. Maybe all will be well.

This race, too, is against the clock. Fifteen contestants. At the far turn is the crucial hang-on spot. The turn can throw a shovel rider askew, a bit like a cue ball caroming against the side rail.

Two of the shovel riders lose it at that corner, but as your son points out, they aren't very big kids. You, one the other hand, are endowed with a solid presence, particularly in the area where your southern exposure meets the shovel.

All too soon, you and Son are up. He instructs you—once again—to hang on with all your might. You can feel him sending out waves of determination and grit. You resolve to hang on.

You assume your monkey position, brace your feet, and take a *firm* overlapping grip on the shovel handle. The starter flag whaps the air. Son's heels thunk into Doodle's flanks and you're off. You clutch the shovel handle and squint like Clint Eastwood as Doodle's hooves throw up clods of what you hope is only dirt. The turf beneath your derriére has turned into a washboard of brain-jiggling bumps. You hunch, head thrust forward, pouring energy into your fingers. Doodle is zooming toward the U-turn at the south end of the arena. Leaning into the turn, you shut your eyes.

You hear yells and screams, many of them yours. You slit open your orbs as your speed increases; you're hurtling forward faster than a politician on the campaign trail. That's when the shovel tips. Somehow you maintain your froglike foot-braced position and cling to the handle. You close your eyes once more.[18]

Doodle thunders on. Your son yells, "Hang on, Mom!"

Terror rides with you. Your hands burn from the death grip on the handle. Then the bucking shovel skews and whacks into the arena's side rail, pitching you clean off the shovel. Your body whips like a flag in a stiff breeze. You know not when Doodle crosses the finish line. You only know your flight has slowed. You can feel yourself sprawled full length. But . . . your hands are still welded to that handle.

From somewhere, maybe another planet, a voice is calling, "Mom! Mom!" You open your eyes. The scenery has quit moving. You ask in a hoarse whisper if it's over.

"Yeah, Mom. You did great. You can let go now."

You lie there, cheek resting against the wood a few inches above the turf. Your hands are frozen. There's no way you can unclamp. Sadly you contemplate spending the rest of your life with a shovel glued twixt your palms.

P.S. You and Intrepid Son win the Shovel Race.

18   It feels safer in the dark.

Part Three

THROWING THE HOULIHAN

Watching an afternoon of team roping is a little like watching paint dry—unless you're a participant. In which case, you and your horse are keen competitors.

55

HISTORY OF THE SPORT
OF RANCH ROPING

*Wherein you learn that while Will Rogers
was called the "Roping Fool," you're pretty sure
you're merely a roping dunce.*

In the early days of cattle raising,[1] doctoring sick or lame critters on the range meant hands-on action. That holds true today as well. Very few cattle can be taught to lie down and stretch out just because a cowboy asks nicely. No, the puncher rides a "ropin' horse" and employs a lariat/lasso/rope to catch and immobilize the cow or calf.

Like many day-to-day ranch routines, ranch roping has turned into a sport with its own traditions, history, and style. As a sport, ranch roping has been around for many years in California, Oregon, and Nevada, but it arrived in Montana through the efforts of Joe Wolters of Grass Valley, California. Joe offered clinics in ranch roping and doctoring.

1   Before four-wheelers, horse trailers, and portable chutes.

The Northern Range Ranch Roping Series (NRRRS) was born in 1999 and now sponsors several roping contests a year around Montana. Their mission statement is as follows: "The goal of the NRRRS is to promote a form of roping that encourages low-stress roping with proper horsemanship and stockmanship, employing a variety of functional and, sometimes, fancy loops. To this end, the NRRRS sponsors ranch roping clinics and events to promote this style of roping."

Contests basically mean a three-man team (or three-woman or a combination of guy/gal) ropes a calf as if to brand or doctor. The emphasis is on safe, easy, and proper handling of the livestock as well as horsemanship. The events are timed; points are earned for fancy or difficult catches. The loops are called "shots." Head shots include the Overhand Shot, the Houlihan Shot, and the Scoop Loop. Heel shots include the Standard Hip Shot, the Straight Behind Hip Shot, the Backhand Hip Shot, the Straight Behind Hip Shot with a Backward Roll, and the Backhand Over the Hip Shot.[2] Skillful roping is an art, and once you understand what's happening, it's thrilling to watch.

While the roping is impressive, it's the ropers who make the event—men and women dedicated to their sport and devoted to the traditions associated with roping. Their credos: Courtesy, Cooperation, Concern, and Respect.[3]

In a ranch roping, everybody gets to participate. That includes men, women, children, the old folks, toddlers, and an enthusiastic audience.

At one end of the arena, blocked off from the main activity, a nine-year-old girl lopes her horse, ponytail bouncing. Outside the arena on the grass in front of the bleachers, three-, four-, and five-year-old kids play like puppies. One pig-tailed urchin has a rope with which she's practicing for her future as a cowgirl. She flips a loop and whether through skill or luck,

2 Sounds like names of country-western songs!
3 Don't worry. There's no end of leg-pulling and joshing that goes on.

she heels a little boy, yanks him off his feet, and snubs him to the fence. They both laugh gleefully.

Under the bleachers a whole platoon of kids of assorted ages are having a dandy time in the dirt. And it's shady under there. From time to time, a kid or two will emerge and go looking for a parent. It's not that the child is insecure and missing Mom or Dad; no, he's merely seeking more coins to make more purchases at the concession stand.

From within the arena a steer—mad and bawling—caught only by one hind leg, comes blasting toward the fence, bucking and snorting trying to rid itself of the rope. A kid of maybe four, on the other side of the fence, jerks off his hat, flaps it, and lisps, "Git back, you old thister."[4]

Ranch-roping competition is done team style, three guys or gals to a team. A calf/cow is chosen by the pull-a-number-out-of-a-hat method; one of the riders must "head" the animal (drop a loop on its head), then herd it away from the bunch; another roper heels the critter and, if all goes well, the cow is put down and stretched out. At that point the third rider (usually the sorriest roper of the team) leaps off his horse, transfers the rope from the bovine's neck to loop a snug noose around the two front feet, then dashes for his mount, curling his twine (his rope) as he goes, and hops aboard; then the total time is noted.

Some teams can accomplish the entire sequence in under two minutes. Some spend all their allotted minutes re-coiling their ropes. Anytime something goes wrong, the announcer feels obliged to tease the cowboy in trouble mercilessly.

Such was the case when Eardly Berdly came a cropper. He'd just completed a really pretty houlihan, catching the animal neatly around the neck, when the cow went ballistic. This was a wild-eyed, dry three-year-old, and she bellered louder

4   Translation: "Get back, you old sister."

than the music kids listen to and about as tuneful. Eardly's horse, Torpedo, and the ballistic bovine did a clever dance, with the horse in the lead. There was going to be one heckuva wreck, so Eardly did the only thing possible: He pitched his rope away from him, but the coils caught on the horn and the taut twine tried to cut off his leg. The situation was not improving. It was time to abandon ship and rethink the situation. So Eardly simply stepped off his horse. Torpedo was really tall—nearly seventeen hands. It seemed to take minutes before the ground met Eardly and flipped him on his face. Quick-thinking Eardly—after he ate his fill of arena muffins—rolled over, leaped to his feet, and bowed to the crowd.

"Ya know, Eard," drawled the announcer, "the way you step off your mount, maybe you should think about gittin' a shorter horse."

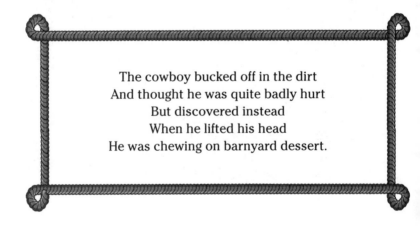

The cowboy bucked off in the dirt
And thought he was quite badly hurt
But discovered instead
When he lifted his head
He was chewing on barnyard dessert.

Horsing Around

ROPES, LARIATS, LASSOS, RIATAS

*Wherein you learn that "twine" is
more than woven string.*

Put a herd of roping cowboys and cowgirls together on horseback in an arena with a bunch of half-grown steers and you've either got a John Wayne movie in the making or a ranch roping. If you're female, you can watch or you can participate.[5]

Often, a roping event is at the local fairgrounds where you will note that the big arena is partitioned off with steel panels that require a lot of upper-body strength to move from hither to thither.

In one end of the arena, a little bunch of steers huddle together, ears and tails flicking nervously. A team of three riders, each swinging a loop, advances upon them.[6] A fourth rider, holding aloft a red-bandana flag, watches, ready to lower it with a snap of his wrist when the team successfully catches the designated animal or times out.

---

5   You'll need a horse, a rope, and a lunatic desire to wrestle a critter heavier than you are.
6   You know that each nervous steer is thinking *don't pick me, don't pick me*.

Judges keep score from their elevated position on a flatbed trailer, parked parallel to the steel-panel partition. A canopy has been erected over the flatbed to keep the judges from melting in the hot sun.

The action in the other half of the arena is a kaleidoscope of color and sound. Dozens of riders mounted on horses—bays, browns, Palominos, grays, sorrels, duns, buckskins—are gathered in conversational groups, or warming up their mounts, or practice-throwing loops.[7]

Ropes, lariats, or lassos are not at all standard, either in lengths or the material they're made from. A twenty-five-foot rope can sometimes leave a roper surprised when the calf he's going for happens to be thirty feet beyond the end of his arm. Sixty feet is pretty much standard among ranch ropers, but length is a matter of preference for most.

Traditional ropes can be twisted fibers of hemp, flax, or other vegetable material—referred to as "grass" ropes. Some ropes are of braided rawhide, some of horsehair, especially popular in the early days. In present times, you can purchase hard-twisted nylon rope.[8] Whatever the construction, ropes were and are essential to a working cowhand.[9]

For an excellent reference on cowboy gear, read *The Cowboy Encyclopedia* by Bruce Grant. "In the old days in the Southwest, a good cowboy was called *uno buena reata* or 'a good rope.' To a Texan, a rope is a rope. In the North, the term lariat is used, a term derived from *la reata*, meaning a rope of twisted fibers. In the Southwest, 'lariat' meant a short stake rope. Cowboys also called fiber ropes a *hard twist, whale line, lass rope, catch rope,* or *throw rope.*

"Fiber ropes range in sizes from three-eighths of an inch

---

7   There's so much testosterone swirling around, you purt near fall in love twelve times.
8   You can even find ropes in assorted pastel colors—in case you're wanting to match your outfit.
9   A rope also comes in handy when hanging villains, outlaws, and rustlers.

to one-half inch in diameter. Smaller ones are used for roping calves and the larger for roping steers and horses. Fiber catch ropes vary from thirty-five to fifty feet in length.

"The reata—often termed 'riata'—is a rope made from four to eight braided strings or 'whangs' of rawhide. This is a rope a cowboy can make himself.[10] A newly made reata is stiff. To soften, it is soaked in warm tallow or other animal oil, then placed around a smooth post and pulled back and forth until it becomes pliable. Reatas are still made, but are now used more for show, hanging from the horn of a fancy saddle, than for practical roping."

Regardless of style, length, or composition of a lariat, it can also be a dangerous tool. If you see a working cowboy who has a hand with a thumb missing, chances are he was attacked by a rogue rope. Ropers can suffer lacerations on their palms, rope burns across their rib-cage areas, or gouges in their thighs, all from having ropes zip, slash, and tear. Some punchers wear light cotton gloves on their rope-swinging hand; some use leather gloves. Most grab on bare-handed. However it's done, roping is a requirement for the working cowhand, or as Bruce Grant put it, "The early cowboy was as helpless without his rope as a hunter without a gun."

10   But not quickly.

A lariat, often they say
When practiced with day after day
Can catch lots of critters
And give them the jitters
But causes one's arm to decay.

THE LADIES AND LARIATS

Wherein you learn that cowgals who rope do it their own way,
and wherein you learn that cowpokes like to watch.

Wild shopping trips, travel to exotic places, mingling with the rich, the famous, and the powerful. That might appeal to some, but for those of us who love horses, nothing could be better than being astride a well-broke horse on a perfect summer day.

The sun shines like liquid gold; the sky is a blue dome overhead; there's no wind; the temperature is just right—not too hot, not too cool; and tall cottonwoods cast comforting shade over the arena bleachers. Twenty-one three-person teams are preparing to participate in a ranch-roping event.

Women ropers bring their own flair to the sport. Your friend, Lulubelle, is teamed up with two men riders. Lulubelle catches the calf critter in a "deep loop," which means that the animal steps through the circle of hemp before the slack gets taken up, resulting in the rope encircling the calf's midsection. This is not a good thing.[11]

---

11   You only lose time and points and annoy the calf.

One of Lulubelle's team drops a second loop around the calf's neck. Lulubelle's job then turns into an effort to remove the "deep loop" off the calf. This is a little like trying to freeze-frame a whirling dervish. The calf dashes and darts. Lulubelle has her hands full trying to dally up her rope to shorten it, so she can get within reaching distance of the leaping, bawling critter. From outside the arena, while she exerts huge effort, other contestants shout advice and instructions. Every rider wants her to succeed. Eventually Lulubelle slips up and pulls off the deep loop, thus allowing the third team member to heel the calf.

It now becomes Lulubelle's job to "tail down" the critter. She must swing off her horse and tie the critter's front legs together while the team roper who's handling the rope on the heel end of the calf keeps the tension just right. (Actually, it's his horse doing the work. A good roping horse is money in the bank. You want one that doesn't blow up just because a rope drags over or under his tail; one that holds steady; one that doesn't give slack until asked.)

When a woman roper is called on to tail down, some roping events allow a fourth person—a guy with that valuable upper-body strength that the gals often lack—to run in to help her tip the animal. But Lulubelle didn't need the help. She gave a yank on the tail; the animal tipped over, but fell in the "wrong" direction. Didn't bother Lulubelle; she merely executed a ballet leap and sailed over the critter to land on the correct side.

Rules say the ground teammate has to remove the rope from around the animal's neck and loop it around its front feet, thereby leaving the animal stretched out between header and heeler for "doctoring" (if out on the range), but not choking the poor thing half to death. Lulubelle accomplishes her task in a flash and the team comes in under the required time limit, thus qualifying for the next go-round.

When asked how she managed to finish up so swiftly, quietly, and efficiently, Lulubelle remarks, "Oh, I just used my cow-whispering voice and whispered in her ear."

Another woman roper, Twilla, is outstanding, not so much for her roping skill as for her dog, Pedro, who accompanies Twilla at all times. Not alongside, but right up on the horse. A weensy Chihuahua the color of charcoal, the little bow-wow perches in Twilla's lap. At times, she plants her front paws (the dog's, not Twilla's) on the saddle horn, stretches to her full height of maybe seven or eight inches, and surveys the crowd with queenly panache.

"Do you put her down somewhere when you swing a loop?" you ask.

"Oh, no, she just crawls around behind me and hangs on."

Then Pedro, on command, demonstrated this skill by slithering away around Twilla's waist to fetch up behind the cantle. You see the little canine's minuscule rear disappearing to the right. In a moment or two, her button-size nose heralds her reappearance from the opposite side. You're pretty sure she winks at you as she resumes her saddle horn throne.

Does Pedro ride along when Twilla actually ropes?

Yes, she does. But she refuses to tail down the calf.

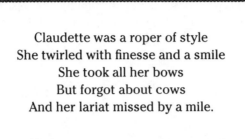

Claudette was a roper of style
She twirled with finesse and a smile
She took all her bows
But forgot about cows
And her lariat missed by a mile.

Part Four

PRANCING AND DANCING

Everybody loves a parade, so they say. You and your horse do too. Dressed in your spiffiest riding duds, a smile pasted on your face, you lift a hand and wave graciously to the watching crowd.

RIDING FOR THE CAUSE

Wherein you learn how to "make a statement" via horseback.

If you're a horse addict, you know that you'll be involved in trail rides, cattle drives, horse shows, and parades. Plus, sooner or later, you'll be involved in a *cause* in which you and your horse will feature.[1]

Such was the case the summer you "Rode for the Montana Cowboy Poetry Gathering" held every August in Lewistown. You hooked up with Tom, another poet/guitar picker/horseman at Garneill, thirty-five miles west of Lewistown. Tom rode from Butte, a distance of two hundred miles from Lewistown.

Because there are few to no horse motels anymore, Tom arranged with ranchers along the route to corral the horses and allow camping spots for the humans.

The day arrives when you are scheduled to meet Tom. You load Buckskin Becky, your mare, into the horse trailer and drive seventy miles to the designated rendezvous. Tom is already there. You have your gear in saddlebags.[2]

1　"Feature" does not mean you're the star of a documentary—yet.
2　Minimal gear: slicker, tennis shoes, Bag Balm, extra toilet paper . . .

Next morning, off you go, leaving your horse trailer with the kindly rancher who ferries it on to Lewistown. Tom leads the packhorse loaded with camp gear.[3] The day turns hotter than John Wayne's shootin' iron. Ninety in the shade. We plod along the borrow pits of the highway. People in cars wave. We wave back. We're smirking proud.

That night's camping is miserably cold. Your supper of Ramen noodles cooked on the weensy butane camp stove does not stick to the ribs. It barely sticks to your throat as it goes down. The night's sleep is constantly interrupted when Tom's two horses and your mare have altercations. They are shut up together in one corral. Becky is low horse on the totem pole and is having the snot kicked out of her. You get up and yell at them, but in a whisper as Tom is sleeping like a stone in his tent.

Next day, it snows.[4] You don layers of clothing, gloves, and earmuffs. Anytime your trail takes you past a business establishment such as a restaurant, a tractor sales company, or maybe just an empty grain elevator, you take advantage of the powder-room facilities.[5]

You reach the edge of Lewistown—finally—and drape signs over the horses' flanks that state: *Riding for Montana Cowboy Poetry Gathering*. You ride down Main Street offering the royal wave to all. A reporter takes pictures.

Tom has arranged for three days' stabling at the local fairgrounds facility. Becky hates that. She spots the trailer and wants to get in.

You have a fine time at the Gathering, reciting poetry and hanging out with other poets and pickers. It's the first and,

3 Since a horse has no pickup bed, stuff has to be carried in panniers hanging off each side of the pack animal.
4 This is *not* a fib. This is Montana where, at the same time, you can have one foot freezing in a snowbank and the other sweating in hot sunshine.
5 The stops are, for you, a necessity. For Tom, not so much.

so far, only time anyone has "ridden for the Poetry Brand."[6]
You're feeling pretty good about yourself until you have a big
wrangle with a primo poet[7] who claims you shouldn't be doing
what you're doing.

His argument:

      a) You're wrong about everything in the universe.

      b) He hasn't given you permission to be an uppity
         cowgal.

Your response:

      a) Say what?

      b) Watch my dust while you try to keep up, Mr. Primo.

Moral: No matter what you do, someone somewhere is
going to criticize.

---

6   No matter what subsequently occurs, no one else can be "first."
7   Just ask him.

For riding way out on the prairie
The facilities tend to be airy
You can bet from the spot
That you've chosen to squat
That your profile will show, so don't tarry.

HITCHING A RIDE

*Wherein you learn how a cowboy
comes to rescue the fair maiden.*

It's Pioneer Day and the parade is scheduled to start at noon. You're among the proud group of equestriennes who love riding a horse in a parade. You wear your best wide-brim Stetson, you sit up tall in the saddle. The saddle blanket is bright red with fringe. The headstall is that fancy one you purchased because of the silver conches and silver inlay.[8] You have braided red tassels in your steed's mane. You are ready to dazzle the populace. You rendezvous in the high-school parking lot where the parade organizers are busily arranging the lineup of floats, vintage cars, little kids in go-carts, fire engines, bands, Legion marchers. . . .

You are on horseback among a group of other riders when you see Lulubelle approaching. She waves. You wave back, pleased that she's noticed how debonair you look. She stands at your horse's shoulder and tells you she has an emergency

8   It cost an arm and a leg, which is why you bought it on the layaway plan.

situation and you must come to the rescue. You groan. You point out that the parade will begin shortly.

She points out that her problem has to do with the parade. It seems that the bird-in-the-gilded-cage person, who was to ride on the events-center float, has become ill, and Lulubelle is looking for a replacement.[9]

Which is how—instead of your spiffy riding outfit—you are wearing a ruffled, flounced, red-taffeta 1890s dress with a plumed hat big as a bushel basket balanced atop your head. A flock of cheery vermilion-red stuffed birds bob among the folds of net decorating the hat brim. You are seated on a swaying perch inside a giant gilded cage suspended from an armature that angles up from the cab roof of a flower-bedecked flat-bed truck. Nestled among the posies is a piano that Lulubelle says she will play while you sing, "She's only a bird in a gilded cage . . ." as the float passes the judges' stand.

You inform Lulubelle that the only song you know about a bird is "When the red, red robin comes bob-bob-bobbin' along." You also inform her that your singing voice sounds like a sick owl.

"No problem," she says. "It'll be awhile before the parade begins. I'll teach you the tune."

You spend the next hour sitting on your bird perch practicing the "Bird in a Gilded Cage" song as Lulubelle plays the melody over and over.

As you shift your weight on your perch you realize you have a problem. "Lulubelle," you rasp in a scratchy whisper. "Lulubelle!"

Lulubelle tips her head back and smiles up at you. "You're doing just fine," she says. "Don't be nervous."

"Nervous is not the problem. I need—"

9   Guess who.

"Remember," Lulubelle warns, cutting you off, "as we go past the judges' stand, you're to sing as loudly as possible."

You plead that you must immediately find a powder room or—your words are interrupted by the growl of the float-truck's big engine.

The parade has started. Lulubelle pretends she can't hear your cries of distress.

The parade's planned route winds for several blocks eastward, then turns a corner, travels for two blocks, and turns again to begin the long trek along Main Street. You remember that Dave's Gas Station occupies the turn at the first corner. Aha. You will merely skedaddle to Dave's, use his facility, cut through the alley, slip back into your birdcage, and be ready to sing your heart out.[10]

Entrance to your gilded enclosure was gained by stepping a short step up from the truck cab's garlanded roof and then into the cage. Egress can be accomplished the same way in reverse, you figure. You can slip out and be back in your cage in moments. After all, the big truck will have to slow down as it maneuvers around the corner.

Gathering up your flouncy red taffeta skirts as best you can, you wriggle through the cage door and onto the cab roof. Hanging on to the armature for support, you slide backward and fumble for a foothold on the truck's window ledge. You grab the side mirror's metal arm and swing, Tarzan-like, to the ground.[11]

Your flouncy red-taffeta dress prevents truly effective fast-track running. You reach the door marked "Ladies" at the side of Dave's service station, grab the doorknob and twist. *Locked!* "Ask Attendant for Key," states a sign in front of your nose. You hobble around and into the station. No one is about.

10 A good general always plans ahead.
11 As you whiz past the window, you catch a glimpse of the driver's face, his mouth a round O of surprise. You don't pause to explain. You're on a mission.

You spot two keys, each dangling from a wooden paddle. Frantically you scoop up the one inscribed with a big black "L" and dart back around the side of the building. At last you manage to open the ladies' room door, zoom inside, fling open a cubicle door. Your relief is nearly faint-inducing, but you dare not dawdle.

Mission accomplished, you grasp the handle of the stall door, which you had slammed behind you. You push. Nothing happens. You pull. Same result. Dear Lord, the latch mechanism has jammed. You rear back and wham the door panel with both fists. Your bird-bedecked hat falls over your nose. Shoving it back, you rub your hands together and hunch your shoulders. Retreating till the back of your knees smack against the toilet bowl, you inhale a deep breath and shoot forward, ramming your right shoulder into the panel. With a sharp crack the door bursts open and you squirt out like sudden ketchup. Only the vanity on the wall opposite saves you from sprawling headlong. Gripping the edge of the sink, you find yourself staring into a mirror. A wild-looking woman peers back from beneath what seems to be a flock of cardinals.

You race out of there and gaze anxiously down the street. You see no sign of a parade. You think you hear faint music of the marching band. The parade must have turned the second corner already! The alley! A short cut! Gathering up your skirts once again, you gallop into the alleyway. If your calculations are correct, you should intersect the parade in the next block.

Because your entire being is focused with burning intensity on getting to the other end of that alley, you don't hear the horseman until he almost runs you down. Without slowing your pace, you glance up into the amused brown eyes of the King of the Cowboys. He rides a white charger, wears an eye-hurting white suit and a snowy ten-gallon hat. Silver sparkles from a gorgeous milk-white saddle.

The vision speaks. "Howdy, Ma'am. Y'all in distress?"

"Not exactly," you gasp. "I'm just trying to catch the parade."

"Well, little lady, so am I. I'd be plumb tickled to offer you a lift."

Your breathing is a wheeze. You are perspiring. At the end of the alley, you can see the parade passing by. You'll never make it in time. You look up at King of the Cowboys.

"Take me to my cage," you plead.

With a smile on his handsome face, King of the Cowboys halts his steed.

You panic as you realize that straddling a horse in your flouncy outfit will be a problem.

"Oh, dear," you whimper.

King Cowboy's smile widens. He leans from the saddle, slips a strong arm around your waist, sweeps you up, and wallops you facedown across the horse's neck—as if you're a newborn calf he's found on the range.

Clamping your hat to your head with one hand, you grip the horse's silver mane with the other. King Cowboy spurs his mount into a gallop. You cling, flopping like a rag doll. Horse, cowboy, and you reach Main Street and the passing parade.

"There! There!" you squeal. "The birdcage! I'm supposed to be in it."

The King of the Cowboys reins alongside the truck and gallantly sets you on the truck bed.

Lulubelle gawks. She's been playing the Bird song for the last three blocks—and wondering why you weren't singing.

"Here," says King of the Cowboys in a John Wayne voice, "is your bird." Then, sweeping his hat from his head, he bows. So does his horse. Your shining white-knight rescuer reins away and gallops off. You gaze after him, paralyzed with love.

"Back in your cage!" hollers Lulubelle. "We're nearing the judges' stand!"

"Yipes," you say, coming out of your trance. You face another challenge. You must scale the wooden backboard behind the truck cab. Leaping up, you hook an arm over the top of the backboard and pull mightily. You achieve the surface of the cab roof, squirm to your hands and knees, and raise your head. The judging stand looms half a block ahead!

Jamming the red-bird hat tight onto your skull, you grab the swaying cage. With enormous and desperate effort, you pull yourself inside and crawl onto the swing perch. You are at the judges' stand.

From below, Lulubelle hisses, "Sing! Sing!" She bangs out the tune.

Your mind goes blank. You can't remember the words! Frantically you try to recall Lulubelle' advice. "It's a bird song," she'd said. "Think about birds."

As the crowd cheers and the judges solemnly gaze, you lift your arms high, grip the bars of your golden cage, and to Lulubelle's piano rendition of "She's Only a Bird in a Gilded Cage," you belt out, "When the red, red robin goes bob, bob, bobbin' along . . ."

RIDING WITH FLAIR

Wherein you learn how to ride in a parade
with panache and queenly gestures.

You're in a parade—on your dancing buckskin mare, Becky.[12]
You've prepared for this. Your saddle has been cleaned and
oiled. Silver conches have been added to Becky's bridle. Red
ribbons are threaded in her mane. A red satin bow is tied onto
her black tail. You and Becky are both *spiffy.* You wear a silver-
belly western hat, white western shirt, bright red wild rag, a
deerskin vest with fringe, ink-black jeans. Oh, m'gosh, if "they"
could only see you now.[13]

As the parade starts, horse riders are assigned in groups
behind certain floats. *Not* the horn-blasting fire truck, *not* the
marching band with flags fluttering—if the flags don't spook
the horses, the sudden din of a Sousa march from a band can
make a horse want to head for the hills—any hills. Likely your

12   She dances because she hates traveling on pavements.
13   "They" being anyone you've ever felt you'd have liked to kick in the hinder; anyone
who's ever snubbed you; or anyone who's tried to intimidate, frighten, or get uppity
with you. (Imagination is a must for horse lovers.)

group of riders is assigned a spot behind something quiet, such as the Edsel Ford belonging to a local collector of odd-ball vehicles.

Do's and Don'ts for how to behave in a royal fashion when riding in a parade:

a) Wear your hat level over your eyebrows. No tipping it back. Tipping back is for wusses, greenhorns, or gals looking to be photographed.[14]

b) Learn the "royal wave." The elbow bends, lifting the hand perpendicular to the body, but hand is not elevated past cheekbone area. Palm of hand is turned toward your body; back of the hand toward the (cheering) crowd. The hand waggles. It does *not* flap wildly. Your waggle and your smile remain reserved and queenly.

c) Paste a Cheshire smile on your face. Look to the right: waggle, waggle. Look to the left: waggle, waggle.

d) When passing the judges' stand, shorten your reins, put Becky on her dancing toes, sit tall, smile, nod slightly, and waggle, waggle.

Sometimes you're in a parade driving Pretty Girl, a miniature horse, behind a two-wheeled cart. Because your hands are busy with the lines, you don't have the freedom to waggle your hand in a queenly fashion. You must nod and smile in a dignified manner. If possible, acquire a small child to accompany you—yours or anybody's. Make sure the kid is dressed to the shiny nines. No sloppy tees or raggedy jeans. Remember, this is the prince or the princess to your queen. Let the child carry a bag of chocolate candies—the ones wrapped in gold foil that resemble large gold "coins."[15] The

14 If the sun is at a particular angle, a photo often shows only the person's lower portion of face; the top is in shadow under the brim of the hat. No matter—keep that wide-brim lid level!

15 Any wrapped candy will do, but the gold "coins" work best as the queen spreads her largesse. (Largesse is not a play on words . . . don't go there).

youngster should do the queen waggle and from time to time toss out candy coins.

WARNING: Toss only sideways or rearward. *Never* toss forward over the top of Pretty Girl's head. She might decide the flying coins are ack-ack flack. Her resulting attempt at a runaway could mess up your rotator cuffs as you pull back on the lines. Therefore, choose your royal kid carefully—one with a good eye and a controlled throw.

It's always good to have someone in the crowd lining the streets assigned to photograph Queenly You as you pass by. When you're in the Home, these photos will stir pleasant memories—perhaps allowing you to imagine you're once again riding your favorite horse instead of a rocking chair.

Part Five

HOWDY, PARDNER

Everybody loves the stories of the West. Which may be why dude (guest) ranches are so popular. Sometimes gal guests sign on hoping to find a willing cowboy. (Generally speaking, cowboys are more than willing to . . . no, let's not go there.) Often guy guests like to stomp around in cowboy boots à la John Wayne.

GUEST METHODS

Wherein you learn how to wrangle dudes and never lose your smile.

One of the ways some "regular" ranches make ends meet is by taking in dudes and letting them "help" with the work of the ranch. While hosting guests is an honorable way of bringing in extra money, herding greenhorns around has its moments. With tongue firmly lodged in cheek, you imagine "brands" to represent styles of ranch guests.

Brand V[1] The guest who insists on vegetarian fare. Usually a female individual, she has no problem "helping" round up the cows while wearing leather boots, riding a leather saddle, and following the south ends of bovines who all wear untanned leather hides. (She doesn't mind eating trout caught in the nearby river.)

Brand P[2] Portly Pauline needs a derrick and six strong cowboys (all maintaining stoic expressions) to hoist her into a saddle. (The ranch keeps a half-Clydesdale saddle horse for such as these.)

1 V for vegetarian vittles.
2 P for pot-bellied, portly people.

Brand W[3] Pitiful Pearl spends her time bemoaning. She's proud to have "low self-esteem." She has saved up a potload of vacation money to come west to a "real ranch" where "real cowboys" can be seen really riding and roping. While she wouldn't admit it, she also yearns to get lucky.[4] She oohs and aahs over all the animals while pretending she's frightened-to-goodness-me. She drives the wranglers nuts.

Brand F[5] The family of five: Mother, Father, college-age Junior and Juniorette, and The Mistake, a kid of eight, conceived after an office party celebrating Dad's retirement.

Much ignored by his family, The Mistake wanders the ranch poking into every activity. The ranch hands—especially Wrangler Sam—take to him, and he to them. They let him tag along doing chores, show him how to halter some of the gentler horses, allow him the privilege of shoveling the horse apples out of the barn, and encourage him in the art of spitting.

The Mistake blooms. His small shoulders square up, he copies his idol, Wrangler Sam, by walking with the stiff, choppy gait of a stove-up bronc buster or a miniature John Wayne.

The day a hundred head of cattle are due to be ear-cropped, The Mistake hangs over the rails, watching closely as a half-moon chunk is snipped from bovine ears.

"Whatcha doin'?" asks The Mistake.

"Well, ya see," says Wrangler Sam, "we don't like to take all of the cow at once fer eatin', so we start out with these bits of ears. We git enough, we cowboys cook 'em up fer ear stew. Mighty good eatin', ear stew. If you've a mind, you kin jist git down here and gather up these here ear pieces 'n take 'em back to the cook. Reckon she'd be plumb grateful. But ya

---

3   W for woe is me.
4   One can only hope some randy fellow will help her out. (So far, no dice—and she's been here two weeks.)
5   F for frisky families.

gotta clean 'em first," warns Wrangler Sam. "Wash 'em good afore you cook 'em."

"Okay," chirps The Mistake and eagerly fills two coffee cans with ear tips; trots back to the ranch house; dumps the hairy, bleeding tabs into the back-porch laundry tub; and proceeds to fill it with very hot water. With a brush, he scours with vigor and verve. Unfortunately, hot water, cow hair, and congealed blood combine to produce a gut-twisting stink. The Mistake becomes nauseous and dizzy.

Wrangler Sam finds him bravely scrubbing away while tears drizzle down his chubby cheeks.

"Shucks, kid," observes Wrangler Sam, "I reckon ear stew ain't on the menu tonight. 'Sides, I got a hankerin' fer ice cream. What's say we give these here ears to Dusty the Dog?"

When Mr. Shakespeare said "All's well that ends well," he might have been speaking of The Mistake and Wrangler Sam. They kept in touch and today The Mistake is the best cow-man in twelve counties and Wrangler Sam is honorary Grampa to The Mistake's seven kids.

HALF DOZEN

ROBERTS' HORSE POWDERS.

PREPARED AND SOLD BY THE PROPRIETOR,

M. B. ROBERTS,

PHILADELPHIA.

SOME GUESTS REQUIRE MORE CARE

Wherein you learn that Scotch is bubbly and how to name a horse.

In your younger years, when customs are traditional, you work on a couple of dude ranches. A male wrangler takes guests on trail rides, flirts with the women dudes, tells tall tales, and participates in the five o'clock cocktail hour with the guests and the ranch owner. You, as a female employee, wash the dishes, make the beds, help cook the food, and *serve* the cocktails at five o'clock.[6]

While a guest ranch must have horses or a fishing stream or both, it might also be a *working* dude ranch. Which means the guests get to "help" trail cattle from here to there, perhaps braver ones can learn to gather eggs, and some may even venture to pull faucets on Bessie the Guernsey.

6　No, you are not privileged to partake of the cocktails (but remember, vodka has no odor and no one can see you sipping if you're behind the kitchen door).

Regardless of the particular style of ranch, every summer produces new dude tales, which provide fodder for stories all winter. Most memorable is Sophie, a tiny, birdlike woman of seventy-three who wears false eyelashes and bats them whenever a man crosses her trail. Sophie *never* misses cocktail hour, during which her lashes flutter up a small breeze.

One afternoon, Sophie fails to appear when the dinner gong sounds. The concerned ranch host tells you to investigate, so off you go to Sophie's cabin. You knock. No one answers, but through the screen door you can hear strange gagging sounds. You enter. The noises seem to be issuing from the bathroom.

"Sophie?" you call.

A figure, garbed in an electric-blue satin robe, appears in the bathroom doorway. A varmint appears to be attacking her face, but then you realize it is only the chin-strap Sophie wears while sleeping to keep her wattles firmed up.

"Are you all right?" you ask.

Sophie's hand flutters, her red-tipped fingernails twinkle like a swarm of ladybugs in flight. One hand pats her throat, from which issues turkey-gobbler gurgles and a froth of bubbles float in the air. Sunbeams brush tiny rainbows in the bubbles. Sophie about-faces and zooms into the bathroom. You follow. This looks serious. You're thinking 911. You find Sophie bent over the sink rinsing her mouth again and again. Finally, she speaks. Pointing to a flask-shaped shampoo bottle, she whimpers, "I thought it was Scotch."

Another dude lady, whom you come to admire considerably, is Paula, a tall, competent, and confident woman, who likes to take early morning walks. One particular morning her stroll takes her past the horse corral where the wrangler is attempting to shoe a horse. The horse objects. It won't stand still; it keeps pulling away; it tries to kneel while the shoer is holding its hoof. Paula pauses and leans over the corral rail to watch.

At that moment a hoof comes down on the wrangler's instep.

"You #$%^&*!!! crowbait, stand still or I'm gonna sell you +(*&^%$#@! for dog food!"

This barrage goes on for awhile 'til finally the wrangler runs out of breath. In the resulting pocket of silence, Paula asks, "You shoeing that horse or naming it?"

A spinster from east in the nation
Saved up for a dude ranch vacation,
But a rhinestone-type cowboy
Found out she know how, boy
So she never left Grand Central Station.

HALF-PINT DUDES
AND OTHER ANOMALIES

*Wherein you learn that sometimes a good horse
is the answer to an irritating problem. And wherein
you learn a song to keep in your heart.*

Going on vacation "Out West" sometimes means staying at
a "guest ranch"—or if you want to be less politically correct—a dude ranch. The summer you help wrangle dudes
provides you with social skills you didn't know you had . . .
such as keeping your mouth shut except for the silly smile
you keep pasted on your kisser. You learn to sling the blar-
ney while at the same time sizing up an individual's horsemanship ability.

There's the guest who claims he's ridden "a lot," which
turns out to be five rides on a rented horse at an indoor
arena. He wants a "spirited" steed. This dude is a Tall Drink
of Water with legs reaching approximately to his ears. You
saddle up Big Ben, a roan seventeen hands tall and equally
as old. Big Ben has never lost a rider. Mr. Tall Drink takes on

a John Wayne swagger.[7] You encourage T. D. to ride around in the corral till you have helped the other guests mount up.

The glamour bedecked little woman is next. She's outfitted in brand-new everything. Her boots have heels so high she walks tippy-toed. A pristine Stetson perches atop her coiffure. She wears painted-on designer jeans. You assign her to Mollie, a bomb-proof little black mare. In a race with a snail, Mollie would lose.

The next would-be cowpoke is anorexia challenged.[8] His name on the registration says Beauregard Butler so of course he becomes Big Bubba to all the ranch hands. B. B. runs his mouth faster than anyone can listen. He has more opinions than a politician running for president. Head Wrangler refers to him as "The Dude from Hell," so naturally you are given the privilege of taking that guest out on a ride. You bring him Boomer, a horse of half-Percheron and half-elephant ancestry. He's big and sturdy enough to carry a circus fat man or twelve children.

Hoisting Big Bubba aboard Boomer becomes a test of strength and sometimes requires an assistant. In Henry the Eighth's time, his minions used a block and tackle and winched Hank aboard. Not toting a handy block and tackle in your pocket, you holler for Head Wrangler, who reluctantly heeds your pleading voice. While you hold Boomer's bridle, Head Wrangler places a shoulder and a hand as a fulcrum under Bubba's derriére and thigh, then shoves upward. If need be, you step to Boomer's off side and yank down Bubba's right foot to meet the right stirrup.

Last to be put in a saddle is little Freddie-the-Fiend. Freddie suffers from A.D.D.—Advanced Dirty Deviltry. His parents have declined to ride, probably just to get free of little Freddie for a few hours. Knowing you will be chief nanny for the day,

7 You just hope he doesn't grab the reins in his teeth and go to galloping hell for leather.
8 He's reached a girth close to that of Henry the Eighth.

97

you mount Freddie on a bay gelding called Cannonball, named because nothing, not even a cannon blast, would upset him.

Once all the guests are aboard their steeds, Head Wrangler leads out—the dudes strung out behind him. You bring up the rear, where you're the designated retriever of anything a dude drops—a camera, a cell phone, a candy wrapper, his or her good sense. You discourage Tall Drink, who wants to race; and calm Ms. Glamour, who is convinced that her horse, Mollie, bucked when the mare was merely kicking at a fly. You encourage Bubba to relax, loosen the reins, and let Boomer do the work. Assure him that Boomer knows his stuff.

Freddie, on Cannonball, treats the horse like he treats his parents. He complains, he whines, he jabs Cannonball in the ribs, he jerks the reins, he slaps him on the shoulder, the rump, he pulls his ears, he's all over the poor horse like flies on scat. You do your best to monitor Freddie, but you can't keep an eye on the little weasel every moment.

For a long time, Cannonball patiently puts up with Freddie's shenanigans. But even good old Cannonball has his limits. As the trail makes a sharp turn through some dense thickets of forest, you temporarily lose sight of the Fiend. But you hear a voice—whining indignantly.

"Help me, somebody help me!"

Rounding the bend, you see Cannonball halted smack under a low-hanging pine branch. Freddie is pasted flat on his back, held immobile by the branch, his spine arched back over the cantle, his head on the horse's rump. Cannonball has all four feet planted, his head is down, eyes half closed. He's had it. This is the first peace he's known during the entire ride, and he's not going to move. Freddie has met his match.

That evening, you give Cannonball an extra ration of grain.

If tolerance leads to wisdom and both are virtues, by the time your summer of dude wrangling is over, you're close to being anointed for sainthood, not to mention Ms. Super Congeniality.

While it's the income from guests at a dude ranch that pays the ranch bills, it's the horses that support the entire operation. Without a horse between your knees, how can you be a pretend cowboy, a make-believe Indian, an imaginary outlaw queen? Horses, like people, come in assorted sizes, shapes, and temperaments. For guests the size of Hulk Hogan, either in actual muscle mass or just mass, Salty, a dappled gray, becomes the horse of choice. Like Boomer, Salty is of draft-horse extraction and can carry four-hundred-pound panniers or four-hundred-pound persons without breaking into a sweat.

The week that guest Sigmund Freud[9] arrives at the ranch, you take one look and immediately press Salty into service. Sigmund—or Siggy, as the ranch hands call him—loves being Out West on a ranch. He loves the mountains; he loves the cattle; he loves the dogs and cats. But most of all he loves the horses with deep and wide affection—as deep and wide as himself. You imagine that it would require a fifty-foot tape to measure Siggy's girth. Salty and Siggy are made for each other.

Siggy spends hours at the corral brushing Salty, feeding him carrots, crooning to him. Salty basks in the attention and soon learns to hang out at the corral gate early every morning. He whinnies when he spots Siggy lumbering across the terrain. You're not sure, but you think Siggy whinnies back. On trail rides, Sigmund rides a custom-made saddle designed on purpose to accommodate overabundant derriéres.[10] To mount "his" horse, Siggy climbs up a wooden stair step; its high point is at about the level of Salty's back. All Siggy has to do is slide across onto the saddle. Siggy and Salty join all trail rides.

9 Sigmund revealed that his parents, Bruce and Bailey Freud, were both psychologists of the Freudian persuasion.

10   A fat lady riding Salty is apt to break into an aria.

You, as usual, ride drag, which often puts you in a position directly behind S. and S. where you can't fail to observe the rhythmic swing of wide haunches—two sets, one divided by a handsome fly-flicking tail.

One morning as you ride your usual rear-guard position, you see an amazing sight. Ahead of you Salty's rump bobs along. On the left haunch somebody has spray-painted the word, WIDE. On the right appears the word, LOAD. It's a moving billboard: WIDE . . . LOAD, WIDE . . . LOAD, WIDE . . . When Siggy discovers his beloved Salty's hinder has been art-decoed, he takes it as a grand joke. As far as you can tell, Salty doesn't take offense either. Sigmund has his picture taken fore and aft with his beloved Salty.

Not one of the ranch hands owns up to the prank, nor do you.

When It's Dude Time in the Rockies

May be warbled. Tune: Springtime in the Rockies.

Now it's dude time in the Rockies,
And the dudes are coming fast,
With their waders and their fly rods,
Oh, they dream of perfect cast.

In their RVs and their trailers,
They are clogging up the roads,
Oh, they park their rigs on Main Street,
And wear shoes with open toes.

And they all have little doggies
That they carry like a purse,
Or they lead big German shepherds,
My, it's hard to say what's worse.

Oh, it's dude time in the Rockies,
And they're coming back this way,
All the travelers from the cities,
With their credit cards they'll pay.

And they love to spend their time at
A dude ranch far from town,
Where the horseys all are gentle,
And the saddles soft as down.

And the wranglers smile to see them
In their funny riding clothes,
For they wear their chaps with nothing,
Leaving birthday suits exposed.

When the tourists come in springtime,
They'll be coming here to play,
Once again we'll say we love them,
While their money flows our way.

And we'll wave good-bye in autumn,
For we're glad they didn't stay,
When it's dude time in the Rockies,
In the Rockies far awayyyy.

Horsing Around

DUDE WRANGLERS HAVE MORE FUN

*Wherein you learn what it means
to do a wrangler's job.*

According to Ramon F. Adams in his book, *Western Words: A Dictionary of the American West*, the word "wrangler" comes from the Spanish *caverango* meaning "herder of the saddle horses."

"The wrangler's job was considered the most menial in cow work, and he did not stand very high in a cowcamp. Yet his job was a training school, and many a good cowboy got his start in a wrangler's job. By studying the characteristics of the various horses, he saved himself much work and grief. He knew which horses were likely to be bunch quitters, which were fighters, and which were afraid of their own shadows."

Adams defines a "dude wrangler" as "a man who serves as a guide to the guests at a dude ranch, usually a former cowboy out of a riding job."

You know you're a dude wrangler when:

. . . on a trail ride, you spend 50 percent of your time picking up hats, coats, cameras, and sometimes teeth that have fallen off the persons of the horseback guests.

. . . on a trail ride, after listening to the dude kids complain they want to run, you finally tell them to "get off and run."

. . . while fording a creek, Baldy, the most reliable horse in the string, decides to lie down and roll, the terrified lady rider gets soaking wet, and it's not all creek water.

. . . a guest thinks a stirrup is an ankle holder and shoves his/ her foot all the way through.

. . . a guest thinks because the milk cow has horns, it's a bull.

. . . when a guest complains 'til you're being driven crazy, you shorten the stirrups on his saddle so has to ride with his legs painfully pretzeled.

. . . when a guest asks, "What's my horse's name?" you tell him/her: "Black Devil" or "White Killer" or "Geronimo," because "he's bucked off so many riders—but he's gentled down some lately."

. . . one of the guest-kids watches while the cow is milked, and he refuses to drink milk ever again.

. . . you explain that the stick-up thing on the front of the saddle is called a saddle horn and the dude immediately says, "Beep, beep."

. . . you watch a dude pick up the reins as though conducting a sing-along, then command, "Go, horse."

. . . a guest insists on wearing his brand-new yellow slicker (it's ninety degrees and not a cloud in the sky).

. . . a guest shows up at the corrals in chaps—but no jeans.

BRANDING TIME

*Wherein you learn that all sorts of folk
want to "help" at a branding.*

Race horses, draft horses, pleasure horses, cow horses, pacers, cart horses, mules, donkeys, burros, ponies, miniatures—whatever the breed, size, conformation, or attitude, horses have jobs. Especially cow horses.[11]

Ramon F. Adams in his book, *Western Words: A Dictionary of the American West*, describes a cow horse thusly:

> A horse the cowhand rides while working cattle. A good cow horse has to possess strength and intelligence, both qualities well trained. He has a natural instinct for sensing direction and detecting danger, day and night. He is game and brave and will drop dead in the performance of his work if need be. He is well adapted to his place, tough and inured to the hardships of his life. His lightness of foot and quickness of motion fit him for the work better than any other type of horse.

11 A cow horse is not a bovine that one rides—unless it's a circus animal.

He soon learns his rider, and they work together. Of necessity he is sure-footed and always has an eye for the trail. He must have good feet, limbs, heart, and lungs, so that he will have endurance; above all he must have good sense.[12]

When it's time to help a neighbor at branding time, you saddle up Becky—a beloved animal, somewhat less exalted than that described by Mr. Adams, but a dandy cow horse—and hie yourself thither.

Brandings usually turn into a neighborhood effort. The women, unless they are riders, ropers, wrestlers,[13] or run the vaccine gun, congregate in the kitchen and produce mountains of food for noon break. This particular rancher has 450 calves to brand the old-fashioned way—rope and drag.

Brandings also often turn into social events particularly favored by city folk whose major exposure to domestic animals is feeding their goldfish. Such was the case with Bob and Bill, two wannabe cowpokes from the city. They hint they want to "help" at branding time. Mr. Rancher figures they might be green but they are big, strong, and eager.

"Sure, come on out," Mr. Rancher tells them. "We'll commence as soon as it's light."

The ranch is so far back in the boonies, it's said air has to be shipped in. To get there Bob and Bill drive two hours on pavement, then travel another long stretch on gravel. When the gravel quits, they follow a bladed track for fifteen minutes and when that ends, there's another three miles to go.

One of them has brought his girlfriend, Matilda. Bawling cows and calves set up a tremendous din. Dust and smoke billows. The smell of singed hair perfumes the air. Half a dozen

12 And then there's the run-of-the-mill steeds you just hope won't buck you off.
13 Not a Jesse Ventura–type sporting event.

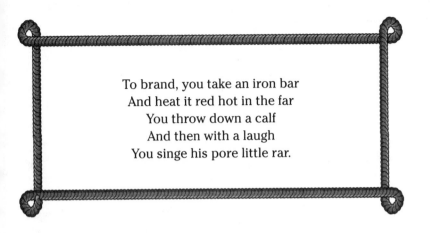

To brand, you take an iron bar
And heat it red hot in the far
You throw down a calf
And then with a laugh
You singe his pore little rar.

ropers swing loops, heel calves, and drag them to a waiting
pairs of wrasslers[14] who pounce, one grabbing the back feet,
another capturing the front legs and holding the head down.
A good pair of wrasslers makes the process swift. In a matter
of seconds, a calf can be branded, tattooed, ear-tagged, vac-
cinated, castrated, and turned loose.

Bob and Bill join in with a right good will while Matilda
(in white jeans) sits on the endgate of a pickup cheering them
on. B. and B. exhibit more enthusiasm than technique. When
a roper drags a calf toward them, they make a swan-diving
tackle and fall on the little critter. Their weight alone pretty
much incapacitates the calf.

Once, making a particularly high dive, Bob grabs a hind
foot and Bill grabs the other hind foot. They hold the poor calf
upended like a wheelbarrow. Competition sets in. Bob and Bill
glare across the calf's back, neither man wanting to be first to
let go.

14   You spell it this way when you're grabbing a calf.

The amused roper, retrieving his rope, asks, "You fellers gonna make a wish?"

As the morning progresses, Bob's and Bill's clean shirts and jeans acquire a fashionable patina of dirt and cowpie stains.

Then a roper makes a high-hock catch. A critter caught high has a lot of leverage. The calf dances around the horse, tries to climb the rope, bucks, bawls, and kicks. Bob and Bill take this as a challenge and soar through the air like Superman and Batman. Their baseball caps fly off and land neatly in the dirt, side by side as if two people have been stomped directly into the ground.

However, the cap owners are too busy to notice such trivia. Bob, who turns out to be bald without his cap, disappears under the calf's belly. The roper, still busily trying to make adjustments in his loop, inadvertently drags the critter along Bob's full length. Bill fares worse. A sharp hoof strikes him in the lip. Blood gushes.

From the sidelines comes a shriek and Matilda dashes into the fray, kneels beside her sweetie, and commences dabbing at his lip with her hankie. She gives him a quick kiss on the cheek. Apparently this furnishes her with an ongoing task because in between the next eight or ten catches, she darts into the field and dabs Bill's lip and smooches his cheek.

Life continues in this rich pattern until noon when a halt is called for dinner. Mrs. Ranch Woman and her neighbor friends have packed up the mountains of food they've prepared and brought it to the branding site. The vittles are served off the endgate of Mrs. Ranch Woman's pickup. After ingesting an unbelievable amount of groceries, the hands relax, stretching out on the ground, making jokes, and recounting the exciting moments of the morning's work, which includes a lot of teasing of Bob and Bill—and Matilda.

"Say, Ma'am," drawls one puncher. "I cut my lip this mornin'. Maybe you could kiss it and make it well?"

Turns out Matilda is a good sport. Getting to her feet, she sashays from one cowpoke to the next dabbing lips—and planting a swift smack on cheeks as well. That afternoon, Matilda takes up wrasslin' calves; her white jeans will never be the same, but she doesn't care.

P.S. About fifteen cowpunchers fall in love.

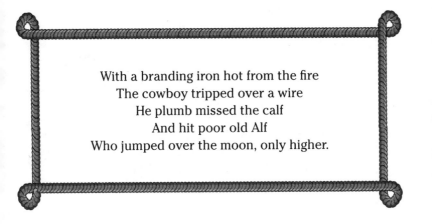

With a branding iron hot from the fire
The cowboy tripped over a wire
He plumb missed the calf
And hit poor old Alf
Who jumped over the moon, only higher.

19

A WORKING RANCH

*Wherein you learn how to use the word "spread"
and that ranch work is not for everyone, and wherein
you learn that a good hand is hard to find,
so don't mess with him.*

Cowboy Smiling Sam signed on as foreman on a ranch owned by Mr. Very Important Person. Mr. VIP had purchased his very own "spread."[15] On his very own spread he installed his very own cows. To help him handle these critters, Mr. VIP looked around for his very own cowboy to help him "work cows"—enter Smiling Sam, an easygoing waddy who has cowboyed with a grin on his face since the age of two. The only thing that really riles Sam is if someone goofs off or gets in the way when working cattle. Sam and his sturdy cow horse, Brownie, make a classy team.

When Smiling Sam and a couple of the boys ride out to bring a bunch of yearlings into the corral, it should be a

---

15   Spread: NOT a condiment used in sandwiches. NOT a description of wide hipbones. NOT telling tales, as in "spreading the word." No, a "spread" is the lingo for expressing the size of your holding—whether five acres or five thousand.

simple job. The pasture isn't large; the corral has been built on purpose next to a steep bluff. Once herded into the small pasture, it's a piece of cake to ease the bunch on into the corral. No problem—unless the cattle spook and choose to scale the practically perpendicular cliff, which would put them into territory from which it would take hours and several good horses to round them up again.

The day is sunny, the temperature mild, the yearlings frisky as popcorn on a hot skillet. The boss, Mr. Very Important Person, shows up on his tall yellow quarter horse. Beside him rides his Very Important Daughter astride her very own high-stepping, high-headed Arabian. Daughter is pretty, single, and says she wants to learn "how to cowboy." All the hands nearly fall off their own horses trying to be first to help her. Smiling Sam also notes the cut of her jib, not to mention the rest of her. His smile widens.

The riders gather the yearlings from coulee, draw, and creek bottom. VIP sits proudly on his big yellow horse, as if leading a charge of cavalry. He blasts through sagebrush, dodges this way and that; he's having a wonderful time annoying the critters.

VIP Daughter sits her horse with supermodel grace; her designer jeans mold to her designer body on her designer saddle on her designer Arabian, causing fanciful designs in the minds of the cowboys—including Sam's.

In spite of Mr. VIP's and Daughter's help, Sam and the boys gather the yearlings, and get them bunched and moving quietly. As they ease the cattle toward the open corral gate, Pretty Daughter gallops ahead, halts smack in the middle of the gate opening, whips out a camera, and shouts, "Daddy, I'll take a picture of you herding your Very Own Cows!"

Yearlings are flighty creatures who have no regard for photographers. This group of bovines goes ballistic, dodges away from the gate, and swarms up the vertical bluff as if they wear suction cups on their cloven hooves. It's an awesome sight. They spill over the top and disappear.

Smiling Sam's internal gunpowder explodes in a mighty roar of expletives that punch visible holes in the airwaves for a full four minutes. He strings curses into complete and complex sentences. He blisters everybody and everybody's ancestry. He uses more words than a dictionary and never repeats. He finishes with terse advice to Pretty Daughter to remove her posterior from the gateway.

How does this story end, you ask?

Smiling Sam and Pretty Daughter are now married to each other. He's pared down his cussing, but she's increased hers.

View by Be

Part Six

WHICH WAY'D THEY GO?

There's a wealth of stories about blunders horse owners make, and you're relieved they're not *all* yours. You've been in a bunch of odd situations on horseback—but perhaps it's best to keep some stories to yourself.

A PAIR TO DRAW TO

*Wherein you learn that knowing one
horse from another is a learned skill.*

Horses: Creatures beloved by many and especially adored
by those who arrive Out West from Big Cities. City slickers
Rosie and Wally[1] bought a "ranch." Naturally, that meant
acquiring saddle horses so they could "ride the range."
Riding the range is a must if you live Out West. It says so in
the Out West Manual.

Eager to learn the Wild West ropes, Rosie and Wally decided
to borrow some horses. They wanted to learn horsemanship
before investing in steeds of their own. Happily, they signed
on with Dan, a local horse trainer who has an arena and some
gentle horses. Rosie picked out a pretty coal-black blaze-faced
mare by the name of Partridge. Wally chose a sturdy bay gelding who answers to Buster.[2]

At least twice a week Rosie and Wally spent hours with
their chosen equines, grooming them, feeding them, checking

1 Not their real names, but it's a for-sure true story.
2 Actually, he'll answer to "hey" if you're carrying a grain bucket.

their feet, saddling up, and finally off they would go riding up cloudy draws. They grew more and more confident of their abilities.

On a particular afternoon, Rosie and Wally drove to the pasture that Partridge and Buster, along with half a dozen other horses, call home. Utilizing a trusty grain bucket Wally caught both steeds, haltered them, and led them to the tack shed where Rosie awaited, curry comb at the ready. She spent a deal of time at the task as Partridge's mane had acquired tangles and burrs. Though tethered to the hitch rack, the mare kept dancing nervously. Rosie was puzzled.

"Something seems to be bothering Partridge," she said to Wally, who was busy sprucing up Buster.

"Oh, she'll settle down," said Wally.

Dan, the trainer, had claimed he'd taught all his mounts to lower their heads for bridling by pressing on the horse's poll. Rosie pressed. Partridge threw her head *up*. Rosie pressed again—and again, and again. After the seventh or eighth press job, she managed to slip the bridle over Partridge's head.

Next came the saddle blanket and saddle. It's not easy to throw tack on a horse that keeps dancing like a ballerina with a sore toe. But Rosie was patient. She kept talking and soothing and finally Partridge stood still.

By now, Wally had finished saddling Buster and mounted up. At long last, Rosie led Partridge away from the hitch rack and prepared to climb aboard. The mare went into another dance routine, this time more of a samba rhythm. Timing her approach, Rosie finally swung into the saddle.

Though Rosie and Wally had originally agreed to ride the range into the hills that day, Rosie had qualms. And Partridge didn't want to leave the barnyard. The mare's samba devolved into a waltz. One, two, three—forward. One, two, three—sideways. Repeat.

"I give up," Rosie declared and dismounted. "You go ahead,

do some riding on your own, Wally. There's something wrong with Partridge."

"Oh, she'll settle down," said Wally. "Here, hold Buster. I'll get on the mare."

What followed was a bunny-hop, minuet, boogie-woogie. Wally dismounted. "Maybe you should just take her back to the pasture," agreed Wally.

Rosie unsaddled. She didn't need to lead the horse; the mare practically dragged Rosie along in her hurry to return. Rosie put Partridge through the gate and was surprised to see another black horse approach, accompanied by a colt.

The colt whinnied, dashed up to Partridge's side, stuck its head under her belly, and began lunch.

That's when Rosie took a look at the *other* black mare— the *real* Partridge.

Later, when Rosie and Wally reported to Dan, the trainer, he drawled, "That was Bessie, the colt's mom you tried to ride. Partridge is her sister. Bessie hasn't been ridden in three years."

VICTORIA'S SECRET

*Wherein you learn that there are many
ways to skin a cat or catch a horse.*

Vicki felt kind of low. The walking plaster cast from foot to early thigh drew lots of attention, but the accident hadn't even been dramatic. How can you brag when you've busted your leg merely by tripping over the garden hose?

But chores still had to be done. As she gimped toward the barn she saw her prize sorrel colt, Firebird, blast through the fence and into the neighbor's field. Sure, wouldn't you know. The best colt on the place tries to play meat-slicer with barbed wire. Horrified, Vicki slid between the barbed strands and hobbled after the colt, hoping he wasn't hurt. She turned once to scream at the house, hoping the man she'd exchanged vows with some years back would hear and heed her howl to bring a halter. Then she limped onward.

The colt, happy as a peach-orchard boar, quit his wild dash and calmly began chomping on the neighbor's alfalfa. Vicki eased alongside and patted Firebird's shoulder. She was

relieved to find he'd not injured himself too badly. A few scratches, a little blood on his chest. He'd heal quickly. By now, Vicki was half an acre away from the barn. Where was Husband? Glancing at the house, a speck in the distance, she saw nothing moving. Hadn't he heard her yell?

Firebird began to mosey away toward the south, where the gate to the alfalfa field stood open. Beyond the gate lay two sections of unfenced pasture. Oh, groan. Vicki needed a halter, a rope, anything. Garbed in plaster-cast-over-jeans and a sloppy sweatshirt, she had not even a belt to use as a substitute halter rope. She almost despaired.

Then inspiration struck, a revelation that could not occur to men,[3] but all women will understand. If you're wearing a baggy shirt, you can disrobe undergarments without ever revealing a thing you don't want to reveal. Here's how: First, you slip both hands under your shirt and behind your back to the hooks holding your, er, womanly garment together and unfasten them. Next, holding your left sleeve with your right hand, you snake your left elbow, arm, and hand backward till the entire limb is completely out of the left sleeve.[4] The sleeve dangles empty. The shirt still covers you like a sack. Inside said sack, you shrug out of the left strap of your, er, womanly garment and allow that to dangle. Slide your left arm back into the shirt's left sleeve. Repeat the above actions with the right shirt sleeve and right strap of your, er, womanly garment.

Vicki completed all the steps for modest removal of underclothing and looped the freed-up garment around Firebird's neck.[5]

---

3   At least, not until after Himself reads this paragraph, but even then the thought won't do him any good.
4   Leave limb attached to shoulder.
5   He didn't care that it was black, lacy, and not push-up.

It took awhile to get home. Had anybody been watching, they would have seen a tall horse and a short woman traveling with a git-along hitch like Matt Dillon's sidekick.

By the time Vicki hitched and teetered back to the barn, her broken leg ached, her arm felt pulled from its socket, but the, er, womanly undergarment held.[6]

About then, her spouse appeared, noticed her, and grinned a big, fat, annoying Cheshire grin. "Hey, Hon," he drawled, "what's that on Firebird's neck? You invent some new piece of horse tack?"

"Yeah," snapped Vicki. "I call it Victoria's Secret."

6   Those things are frilly for looks, but hell for stout.

HOW TO BE A HELPING HAND

*Wherein you learn how to become an assistant
to a ticked-off friend in need.*

The phone rings. "Would you have time to come out and feed the livestock this afternoon?" asks your friend, Lana, the dude ranch operator. "My husband's out of town and I've had a slight accident."

"What's the problem?"

"I'll tell you when you get here."

Any time Lana refrains from direct commentary, you know there's going to be a good story forthcoming. Her guest ranch is a ways out of town. You find her in the ranch house living room looking downright peaked. She is swathed in an interesting arrangement of Velcro straps and buckles.

"You look packaged for shipping," you say.

"Thanks," says Lana, wiggling the fingers of her tied-down right hand in a rather rude gesture. Wiggle is as much as she can accomplish because of the sling that holds her shoulder and forearm immobilized as if she is hugging herself.

"Are you in pain?"

"Only when I breathe or move or think."

"So what happened?"

"My husband's horse happened. He dumped me."

"Mortimer? The equine with the ambition of a dust ball?"

"That's the one. I was taking some guests on a trail ride around the north section of the ranch. Usually I only let guests ride in the arena until they prove they are experienced riders. They said they were experienced. They even brought their own horses. So I agreed to take them out on the trails."

"The story's getting better. Tell all."

"We were going up the steep part of the trail single file. I was last in line behind one of the guests. She was mounted on a nubile young mare. That's when Mr. Mortimer fell in love." Lana shifts her weight and winces.

"Oh, no!" You picture a *Horse Whisperer* catastrophe. "Did your guests get hurt?"

"They didn't even know what was going on. Mr. Mortimer tried to rear; I pulled him back; he toe-danced on his hind legs, came down on his front feet, and catapulted me like a green apple out of a slingshot onto a pile of rocks. I harrowed the big stones into little pebbles with my shoulder."

"Ouch," you say.

"You can say that again."

"Ouch," you oblige. "You must have felt really silly in front of your guests."

"They didn't know until they turned around that I wasn't right behind them. Mr. Mortimer just stood there looking at me like a talk show host with amnesia. I managed to remount and then told the guests I was expecting a long-distance call back at the ranch."

Lana sighs again and winces again. "I put Mr. Mortimer in horse jail," she states through gritted teeth. "He's still in the stall."

"You want me to turn him out?"

"Turn him out, turn him loose, turn him into dog meat for all I care," says Lana and reaches for a pain pill.

When riding a bucker, take pains
To keep careful hold of the reins
Or else try some glue
Twixt the saddle and you
Lest the maverick scatter your brains.

THE HOARSE WHISPERER

Wherein you learn that mules are smarter than the average rider and that mule trainers don't whisper.

When Robert Redford filmed *The Horse Whisperer* in and around your town, the jokes flew like a hatching of caddis flies. Whisperers popped up everywhere.[7] There were Sheep Whisperers, Hog Whisperers, Cow Whisperers, Chicken Whisperers, and most fanciful of all—Mule Whisperers. The main difference between whispering to a horse and whispering to a mule is that mules pay no attention to whispers. A mule whisperer must yell and is therefore referred to as a mule yeller. Mule yellers' voices don't last long; they become raspy as rusty saws and finally, tragically, fall entirely mute.

Probably the best-known mule yeller in the country is Joe-the-Mule-Yeller, who has his own television advice show. Joe decided to produce a film on mule yelling. He searched for the perfect screenplay and finally located one in an abandoned corral after a heavy rain washed away a pile of stud

7   A little like those ubiquitous Elvis impersonators.

droppings. The story deals with a man of extraordinary talent in the art of handling mules with problems.[8]

When Robert Redford wanted to option Joe-the-Mule-Yeller's screenplay, Joe figured he himself was a natural for the part of Old Hoarse Yeller, the tough, yet kindly, man who teaches mules to be nice.[9] A kindly widow woman who loves mules and men comes to Joe with a problem mule. The critter has stepped in a badger hole and has developed a severe allergy to holes. Should he spy one, he goes berserk, kicking, bucking, pitching, and braying.[10] Joe ponders the problem, advises the widow, cures the mule, and then in a twist of irony, Joe gets kicked to death. But he leaves all proceeds to the widow. The film is also a musical. Joe-the-Mule-Yeller composed the theme song himself. The CD is available at local stores and on BlackBerrys and iPods.

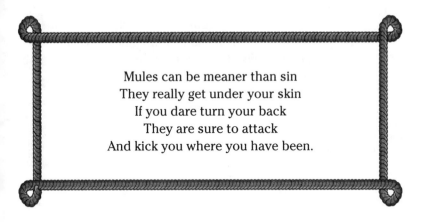

Mules can be meaner than sin
They really get under your skin
If you dare turn your back
They are sure to attack
And kick you where you have been.

8   A mule, by definition, is a problem; working with them requires courage of the nutmost.

9   Joe stands taller than Robert, but his head is smaller due, it's said, to being kicked too many times.

10   This makes for an uncomfortable ride.

Old Hoarse Yeller

Tune: Home on the Range

Oh, give me a home where long-eared mules roam,
And the gophers and coyotes play
Where always is heard a discouraging word
And the skies are real cloudy all day.

Chorus . . .
Home, home on the range,
Where the mules and the jackasses play,
Where Hoarse Yeller yells in stubborn mule ears,
And he's hoarse cuz he's screaming all day.

Now Hoarse Yeller knows how to cure all the ills
Of a mule with emotional scars,
He shrieks in its ears and shares the mule's fears,
And he feeds him on chocolate bars.
Chorus . . .

Now often at night when things don't go right
Cuz the mules are ornery as sin,
Old Hoarse Yeller moans and swabs his sore throat
With some lemon and bourbon and gin.
Chorus . . .

Where the prairie winds blow, the zephyrs so fierce
The breezes so rainy and wet
That Old Hoarse Yeller groans bout his home on the range
Where a mule makes a god-awful pet.
Chorus . . .

Oh, we love cactus flow'rs on this prairie of ours
The mules they heehaw and bray,
We get bucked on our heads and must go to bed
To heal up and start a new day.
Chorus . . .

TEETER-TOTTERING

Wherein you learn how to unhitch a
trailer without using your hands.

Horses can be trained to do wondrous tasks. They can be taught to kneel or even lie down to allow, say, a disabled rider to mount. They can be taught to leap off a tower into a tank of water. They can be trained to count on command. They can learn dressage, side passing, pacing, high stepping, and, as every good hand knows, nothing beats a well-trained cutting horse. Horses will jump over ditches, hedges, and convertibles. They will pull carriages, logs, plows, sleighs, and—in the days before horseless carriages—fire engines and freight wagons. Horses have carried men into battle, knights in jousting matches, and Lady Godiva in the buff.[11]

But, as far as you know, your mare is the only equine who has learned how to teeter-totter.

It begins as a simple chore. Move the horses from pasture A to pasture B by loading them into the horse trailer and driving them a mile and a half up the road. The day is warm,

11   When she finished that ride, she must've itched something fierce!

though wind gusts hit cyclone speed from time to time. Just holding the trailer door open requires assistance, so you call on your friend, Bethel-from-California.

"Sure, I'll help," says Bethel. "You hitch up and I'll meet you at the pasture."

You attach your beat-up two-horse stock trailer[12] to your pickup. The first candidate for transport is Becky the mare. All of her life she has ridden happily in long, four-horse trailers, but she hates short ones and has been known to express her disapproval with thunderous, unladylike fits of kicking.

To be on the safe side, you decide to haul Becky by herself and make additional trips for the others. With the help of a small pile of oats you place inside the trailer as a bribe, she loads just fine.[13]

With Bethel-from-California following in her own vehicle, you start down the county road. At the turn-off onto your lane and only a quarter mile from your horse pasture, the first inkling that something is out-of-kilter occurs. A huge thud followed by a resounding bang causes you to mutter, "Oh, groan, the mare has decided to go hysterical."

With true cowgirl logic, you figure maybe Becky will settle enough to reach the pasture if you *go like the devil before things get worse*. Things get worse. You fly over potholes the size of asteroid craters. In your rearview mirror, you see the trailer heave up, then surge down accompanied by ferocious clanks and horrible thumps. You can see the mare's head lift and drop as the trailer nose flies up, then plunges down like a boat in a stormy sea. With more true cowgirl logic[14] you leap to the conclusion that the mare is rearing and striking, then bogging her head and kicking with both hind feet, causing the trailer to teeter up and totter down.

---

12 An outfit so old, it once was used to carry small dinosaurs.
13 Bribery is only immoral among humans (unless it's a politician, then it's a given).
14 Cowgirl logic: A true cowgirl never hurts herself if she falls on her head.

You take the turn onto the gravel path leading to the corral, the final approach; only a few hundred yards to go on a downhill slope. That's when the trailer catches the pickup and bites it in the behind. You brake to a stop. "Shoot," you mutter. That darned mare has bounced the trailer off the hitch. You emerge from the pickup to inspect the damage.

It is then you discover the truth. The mare is not even excited. She hasn't been kicking. She's been too busy keeping her feet planted as she rode the teeter-tottering trailer, which was being dragged along attached to the pickup bumper only by the safety chain.

Bethel-from-California pulls up behind you, gets out of her vehicle, and for a moment you wonder if she's sick. She doubles over, gasping and clutching her stomach; her face acquires an interesting, somewhat mottled shade of red. When she finally catches her breath and stops choking with laughter, she observes, "So, this is the way you haul horses in Montana?"

It is another true cowgirl moment—a really embarrassing one.

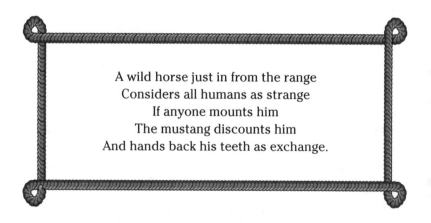

A wild horse just in from the range
Considers all humans as strange
If anyone mounts him
The mustang discounts him
And hands back his teeth as exchange.

THE HORSESHOER

Wherein being nice to your horseshoer is primo, as well as highly entertaining.

Today is Monday. The horseshoer arrives to trim seven horses' feet—six of the steeds are yours and one belongs to a neighbor. The day is gorgeous—sunny and warm—too warm for this time of year but no wind. A day without wind is a day to treasure.

The horseshoer sometimes has a partner with him, a cowboy (call him Ernie) with a flair for shoeing and training horses. While Ernie loves working with horses, he's severely allergic to any other kind of ranch job.

Today, the shoer (call him Bert) faces the shoeing task on his own, which means you stand around holding halters attached to horse heads and conversing about this and that—sometimes with the horse, but mostly with Bert.

"Where's Ernie?" you inquire.

"Well," drawls Bert from his position bent double while holding a miniature horse hoof, "I haven't seen him lately, but I think he had a bad job scare last time we worked together."

"Job scare?"

"Uh, huh," says Bert as he rasps a hoof, "Ernie and I were at a big ranch shoeing some thoroughbreds. The ranch owner's trainer had just quit. When he finds out Ernie is a skilled horseman, he offers him a job. Tells him all he has to do is work with horses. Ernie starts to get interested. So, I sorta mention to Ernie that it's a pretty big ranch. Lot of hay ground. He might have to do some irrigating."

"Oh, yeah? Did Ernie take the job?" you ask.

"Well," Bert says, "the owner is a-leaning on the top rail of the corral. When he hears what I say, he quick tells Ernie that the ranch has a hired hand do that kind of job. So, I sorta mention how a ranch that size has a whole lot of fences. The owner admits the ranch has 'bout sixty miles of barbed wire. But he tells ol' Ernie the ranch hires a rider to take care of fencing and repairs."

Bert straightens up. Looking off at the peaks of the far mountains, he says, "Ya know, Ernie commences to get a worry wrinkle cross't his forehead. He starts kinda sidling away. The ranch owner sorta lifts his voice some to tell Ernie the ranch pays real well. Would furnish a house, grub, and gas for Ernie's pickup. And time off whenever he wanted."

"So, what did Ernie do?" you ask.

Bert bends to his shoeing task again. "Well, I sorta brought up the fact that the ranch runs three or four hundred head of cattle. Cows, mostly. So I remind Ernie that come spring, he might have to help out with the calving. Rancher guy jumps in, claiming the ranch hires calvers for that job. By now, ol' Ernie has kinda backpedaled way over by the corral gate."

"Maybe they got a feller doin' the calvin' Ernie," I says, "but what happens when one of the hands quits?"

Bert turns loose your little horse, and you hand him the lead rope attached to horse number three. "So, what did Ernie do?" you inquire.

"Ya know," drawls Bert, "Ernie's kinda spooky. He kinda oozes outta the corral and backs up 'til he bumps into the pickup. He sorta slithers inside the cab and hides there.

"'Bout then the ranch owner asks, 'What's the matter with him? Is he sick?'

"So I hadda tell him, 'Well, I think ol' Ernie just had a job scare.'"

A day without wind is a treasure. A day with no wind and a storytelling horseshoer is a double bonus.

HERE COMES SANTA CLAUS

Wherein you learn that Santa arrives on time.

In the dusk of the December evening, your snow-blanketed barnyard looks like a charcoal-drawn Christmas card. Your friend Lulubelle is helping you adjust the harness and sleigh bells on Doodle, your family's misty-eyed bay workhorse.[15]

"You've just *got* to do it," Lulubelle pleads. "After all, it's CHRISTMAS. You can't let everybody down!"

Lulubelle is laying a guilt trip on you on behalf of the annual Community Hall Christmas party. Santa Claus is usually Hank Murston. Disguised in a cherry-red flannel suit with cotton trim, Hank lugs a bulging sack into the hall and dispenses gifts and goodwill with the enthusiasm of a manic giant.

"Hank Murston," Lulubelle wails, "is down with lumbago and *someone* has to be Santa. You're the only person who can do it. The men are all at the hall putting up the tree and decorations."

Lulubelle chokes on held-back tears. You moan as you continue strapping a set of elk antlers sprinkled with Christmas

---

15 Doodle will put up with *anything*.

tree lights onto Doodle's head. Battery-wired lights blink on and off like fireflies. You inform Lulubelle you are taking kids for sleigh rides as you do every year. But you can't be Santa.

Lulubelle insists, "There's absolutely no one else available to be Santa. Surely you wouldn't disappoint the children at Christmastime." Her voice breaks again as she inserts a small sob. "We must have a Santa for the kiddies."

You argue that if it's so important, why doesn't she—Lulubelle—do the Santa samba?

Lulubelle responds that it's obvious. You're the one with the horse and sleigh. She rattles on.

"I just know," she says, her voice as husky as the winner of a hog-calling contest, "I know you won't let the community and the children down."

You protest weakly that you're way too short to be Santa and your voice is way too high.

Sensing victory, Lulubelle claps her hand on your shoulder and looks deeply into your eyes.

"Oh, you'll be just fine. You can sing and shout as you drive. That'll roughen your vocal cords, make your voice husky. It's a fine thing you're doing," she intones solemnly, then hands you a Santa suit.[16] "Just put it on over your regular snowsuit."

Surrendering completely, you slide into a pair of huge baggy red pants and draw them up and up and up. You run out of trouser material at nose level. Hank Murston is six foot four. Just his legs are taller than you.

"We can fix that," says Lulubelle, yanking the seat cushion off the sleigh. "We'll stuff you with this to take up the slack."

The cushion is a flat, stiff, horsehair chunk, a foot across and three feet tall. Lulubelle arranges the pad up and down the length of your person and secures it with many coils of

16 Lulubelle never doubts her powers of persuasion.

bale string. The cushion bangs your kneecaps at the lower end and props up your chin at the top.

Lulubelle holds Santa's coat so you can slide your arms into the sleeves. A foot of empty cloth dangles below your mittens. Ever resourceful, Lulubelle hitches up the sleeves with baling-string garters. The coat's fur-trimmed hemline flaps nearly to your ankles. Lulubelle solves that by cinching up your waist with a wide black Santa belt, blousing the jacket over the belt.

"Now," she orders, "stick your pant legs inside your four-buckles."

You point out that you can't bend in the body cast she's placed on you.

"Let me help you," says Lulubelle. She guides you as if piloting a robot, backing you against the sleigh. You brace, spread-eagle fashion. Kneeling like a worshiper in the snow, Lulubelle stuffs the balloony flannel legs of the Santa pants into the tops of your four-buckles. Then she bounces to her feet and hands you a white woolly thing.

"Your beard," she declares, and hooks you into flowing white whiskers—which hang to your knees. Over your head, Lulubelle yanks a curly white wig with a tasseled red cap.

You mention that if you fall down in this straightjacket outfit, you'll die because you won't be able to get up.

"Nonsense," Lulubelle sympathizes. "I'll help you board your sleigh."

Lulubelle positions herself at your posterior and hoists. Somehow, you manage to lever your incredible bulk into the sleigh and fall back onto the seat. Lulubelle places the driving lines into your mittened hands.

"There you are," she says with ghastly cheer. "I've put the sack of gifts in the sleigh, so all you have to do is remember to carry them into the school. See you at Community Hall. I'll save you some hot-spiced cider. Merry Christmas!" Without a backward glance she dashes to her pickup, hops in, and drives away.

With a sigh and an inner resolve that you will somehow get her for this predicament, you flap the driving lines and patient Doodle leans into the traces. The sleigh moves forward, whispering two thin tracks through the snow. You pop the lines again and Doodle breaks into a trot, setting the sleigh bells jingling merrily.

"HO! HO! HO!" you bellow as the sleigh sweeps around a snowy bend. The carriage lanterns throw alien shadows around Doodle and the sleigh and you. But there is no wind, the moon casts silvery light, and the air is filled with the blue magic of a snowy winter night.

"Jingle bells, jingle bells," you sing, as happy as if you had good sense.

Black stick shapes of a fence stretch parallel to the road. Doodle trots on, brisk as a colt. You fly onward for quite a while, and then a while longer. You begin to feel an uneasy twinge up your spine. You stop singing. Oh, dear, have you turned the wrong way at that last section corner? Should you turn around? But where? The road is barely a one-way path between snow-filled borrow pits. You don't want to get stuck in a drift. You'll have to keep going till you locate a wide spot.

You strain to see the road ahead and barely make out the black shape of a windmill. Sheep Johnson's windmill. Oh, good. The Community Hall is only a short distance beyond.

You ponder Sheep Johnson. Sheep keeps to himself. Not exactly unfriendly, but he sure doesn't go out of his way to neighbor. Some folks say he's an old-time remittance man and others hold that he's run away from a blighted romance. He ignores all invitations to join in Christmas fun. It's a shame. But Sheep lives only a half mile from Community Hall, so you figure you'll soon be at the schoolhouse. You relax.

"Here comes Santa Claus, here comes Santa Claus," you warble. Then you spot a light yonder. A dog barks. Doodle breaks into a lope, whizzes through an open gate, and halts before a small frame house with a narrow wooden porch jutting from the front. This is definitely not Community Hall.

The overhead yard light spotlights you and Doodle as the door of the house pops open and a barrel-chested individual— at least twelve feet tall—stands framed in orange light.

"Oh, wow," you whisper, "I've goofed."

A voice that sounds like an irritated grizzly bear growls, "WHAT'S GOIN' ON OUT THERE?" Then the voice adds, "SHUT UP, JEZEBEL!"

You know the yeller doesn't mean you because the dog quits barking. You also know that Doodle has taken you through Sheep Johnson's open gate right to his front door. Yikes. Oh, well, it's Christmas. Most folks are nice at Christmas.

"Hello, there, Mr. Johnson," you sing out. "Sorry to bother you. Just wanted to turn around in your yard."

"WHO'S THAT?" bellers Sheep Johnson.

"Er, it's Santa Claus," you say. "I'm on my way to the Community Hall Christmas party."

Sheep Johnson's impressive mustache twitches. Then it twitches some more and finally his teeth appear in a grin wide enough to make a jack-o'-lantern proud. In another moment, he throws back his head and a strangled noise emerges from his throat. You realize Sheep Johnson is laughing.

Still chortling, he plods down the porch steps, inspects Doodle's blinking antlers more closely, then breaks into another fit of laughter. "I hear tell," he rumbles, when he catches his breath, "that women are doing everything nowadays—but Santa Claus?" He slaps his knee as another fit of amusement overtakes him.

At that moment, you want to kill Lulubelle. This is her fault. She is waiting warm and comfy at the Hall, while you sit like a store dummy in a baggy Santa suit feeling like a dope. Sheep Johnson keeps on with his uncalled-for merriment at your expense. Definitely you are going to kill Lulubelle. Then, as Sheep's raucous throat-noise continues, inspiration strikes.

"Mr. Johnson," you say, making your voice firm, "you're absolutely right about the inappropriateness of a woman Santa Claus. That's why I've stopped here."

"Huh?" he says.

You wrap the driving lines around the brake handle, maneuver your stick legs around and prepare to descend. Your body, splinted against the stuffing pad, slides like a hunk of scrap iron off the sleigh and you pitch forward. With your face in the snow, you wonder if Lulubelle would be sorry if you suffocate. You try to rise, but the best you can do is roll over on your back.

Sheep Johnson towers above you like a skyscraper on legs. By now, the man has tears streaming from his eyes as his merry appreciation continues. Gulping a couple of times, he reaches down and scoops you to vertical.

"Thank you," you say. Then briskly, "You've got ten minutes to change into Santa."

"Huh?" His laughter vanishes.

You begin stripping. You toss him the hat, wig, and beard. You unbuckle the belt, skin out of the jacket and the seat cushion, sit on the sleigh's step, and pull those voluminous red pants out of your four-buckles and slither them off. Wadding up the garments, you shove the whole pile at Sheep Johnson's chest. "Go. Get dressed. I'll wait here. I'm your designated driver."

Twenty-three minutes later, you halt Doodle at the hitch rail in front of Community Hall, hop down, tie the lines to the rail, and skedaddle inside, banging the door behind you.

A gaggle of children and adults are busily draping popcorn strings, icicles, and angel cookies on a tall pine tree. Several mothers are busy in a kitchenette at the far end of the

building. Lulubelle, her back to you, is hanging a candy cane on a branch. Hearing the door slam, she calls out in falsetto, "My, is that Santa's footstep I hear?" Then she turns and her expression takes a dive. White-faced, she leaps to waylay you in the middle of the long room. Nearly in tears, she gasps, "Oh, no. Oh, NO! I can't believe it. You've let me down. Where is your Santa suit?"

"I gave it away," you answer solemnly. "It just wasn't me."

Lulubelle's face begins crumpling as she tries to decide whether to cry, scream, or hit you.

At that instant, from outside the hall comes a deep rolling bass "HO, HO, HO! MERRRRRY CHRISTMAS!"

Every child in the room freezes as if bewitched. Into the silence another bellowed "MERRRRRY CHRISTMAS!" shakes the building. Then the kids break, sprint for the door, and fling it wide.

Through the open portal, you see a big bay reindeer with blinking antlers tethered to the hitch rail. An enormous bearded figure, dressed in cherry red, leaps off the sleigh and heaves a bulging bundle to his shoulder. "MERRRRRY CHRISTMAS!" he roars as he stomps onto the porch and through the door. The smaller children fall back in awe while some braver ones shriek, "SANTA CLAUS! SANTA CLAUS!"

"Who," squeaks Lulubelle, "is *that*?"

"Well, it's not the Lone Ranger," you murmur as Santa strides to the Christmas tree.

Angling two ham-size hands on his hips, Santa faces the assemblage and once more roars a Christmas greeting. Then he opens up his bundle, reaches in, and draws forth the first brightly wrapped package.

Throwing an arm across your shoulders, Lulubelle bends her blue-eyed gaze upon you. "I knew you wouldn't let me down," she whispers. "He's perfect. Er, who is he?"

"Santa Claus," you say. "Got any of that hot-spiced cider left?"

Part Seven

ON THE TRAIL

There are trail-ride groups all over the country. You can join a wagon train and ride from point A to point B, C, or the whole alphabet. You can follow Chief Joseph's Trail, the old Bozeman Trail, or a jillion other choices. Try one. Remember, when you're in that home in that rocking chair, you'll want to think back on the great days with your horse.

RIDING THE TRAILS

*Wherein you learn how to behave on trail rides,
and wherein you learn how to apply Bag Balm
discreetly, sometimes while mounted.*

When the opportunity to ride with a modern-day wagon train comes along, you don't hesitate. You load Becky, your buckskin mare, into your horse trailer and tally-ho. You are going to relive the "old days." You're going to lope across prairies, ride up cloudy draws, ford streams, sleep under the stars, eat vittles cooked over hot coals, and tell tall tales around evening campfires. You're an "outrider," which means you're not attached to or driving a wagon. No, you'll be in the saddle all day, keeping a keen eye on the horizon for possible hostiles or handsome strangers.[1]

Your gear includes a bedroll, which in early cowboy days was called a "sougan." To make a proper sougan, fold a number of blankets lengthwise, overlapping them so you end up with a sack open at each end; then fold all in a piece of canvas like a pita sandwich. You are now ready to enjoy your night

1   If you find one, keep him to yourself.

under the stars, and since your outer layer is canvas, you'll stay dry if it rains.[2]

One wagon has been designated to carry bedrolls and tents; you carry personal gear in saddlebags. On a several-days' trail ride, you can't have too many saddlebags—the banana bag behind the cantle,[3] the small double bag over the saddle horn,[4] and the double bag over your horse's hindquarters.[5] Of course, your pockets contain necessities such as lip balm, Bag Balm (you can get weensy cans of this balm at the feed store), at least *one* packet of tissue for emergencies besides your runny nose . . . don't ask what the "besides" means.

Your bigger saddlebags harbor an extra shirt, a pair of sneakers,[6] basic toiletries, a watermelon-pink bathrobe, and the snake-bite medication of your choice.[7]

Camp food varies in quality according to who's doing the cooking. Sometimes there's a camp cook—depending on the size of the group. If it's a biggie with hundreds of riders, the entire ride will be organized to the last detail. There will be a mess tent, and you can pretty much count on getting enough to eat.[8]

If you're with a bunch of rider friends going on a two- or three-day jaunt, maybe one of you will assume Cookie's duties. If you have pack horses, they carry gear and foodstuff. Once in camp, everybody pitches in, collecting firewood, setting up tents, tethering horses, feeding horses.[9] Whatever you plan

2 Yeah, right.
3 In this one, carry your toilet paper and lunch.
4 In this one, carry your camera, extra tissue (your nose will run at inopportune moments), and your Last Will and Testament.
5 In this one, carry all the big stuff you won't need 'till it's time to fall in the sack.
6 These are your camping "bedroom slippers" for those times when you must get up in the night and go searching for a powder room.
7 This is an oral medication to be taken nightly during tall-tale tellings around the campfire. Dosage up to you, but moderation advised.
8 However, always carry Snickers bars or snack of your choice.
9 No whining allowed.

for meals, *always, always, always* take plenty of coffee—the leaded kind.[10] Once, when coffee was forgotten, the forget-tee nearly suffered a lynching, saved only by his obsequious pleading. Also, the ride was crossing open prairie—no handy trees.

Try not to be in charge of making the coffee, but should the task fall to you, remember there are no electrical outlets in camp. You have to make "cowboy coffee" in a big enameled bale-handled pot.

Basic Joe

A pound of ground coffee per gallon of water. (Or a heaping tablespoon of grounds per cup of agua.)

Stick the pot over the fire and bring the water to a rolling boil.

Remove pot from fire. Add the coffee. Put pot back on fire.

The moment it begins to boil again, take it off the fire and set to one side over some coals to keep it warm without bubbling.

Let it stand for a few minutes, then add a little dab of *cold* water to make the grounds settle to bottom of the pot.

Some people go the fancy coffee route by adding an egg in or out of the shell, or eggshells, or a raw egg—sep-arating white from yolk and adding one of the parts.[11] You can bother with that if you want to. Julia Child and Martha Stewart have no written rules on camp-coffee fixin'. Neither have the cowboys. Coffee-making variations are merely left-over traditions. The main thing is to make it strong. To look

10   Decaf is for wussies.
11   Somebody had too much time on his/her hands.

forward to that first morning sip of hot, black java and then discover it's weaker than tea made from previously used tea bags is enough to spoil the entire day. The disappointment could drive you into therapy.

Care of the coffeepot is pretty easy. Don't wash it. Ever. You can *rinse* it a little just to get the yucky used grounds out, but don't be soap-scrubbing the pot.[12]

Besides the obligatory coffeepot, the cooking vessel of choice is a Dutch oven—an iron kettle with a lid. Sometimes a Dutch oven has legs, sometimes not. Leggy pots can be set right over the fire on the ground. No-legs pots can be hung over the fire with one of those S-shaped hangers—stiff wire gizmos with a hook on each end. Picture a sawhorse over a campfire and pots dangling from the crossbar of the sawhorse. No! No! Don't use a *real* sawhorse. Make something similar out of sticks. Make the crosspiece high enough to allow room for pots to hang down over the fire, but not so close you burn up the outfit.

On the other hand, don't make the thing so high you have to use three hooks linked together to allow the pot to dangle somewhere close to the fire. The stick made-on-the-spot unit is real romantic and woodsmansy and written about in survival manuals. But it's a lot easier to make one at home out of steel rods that you can take apart and carry on your horse.[13]

Maybe the finest aspect of a trail ride happens around the campfire. You've spent the day in the saddle, you've filled

12 To do so causes the earth's platelets to shimmy. You don't want to cause a quake in California.

13 There are a bazillion books on camp cooking, trail ride food, outdoor do-it-yourself gear, and the like. Buy at any bookstore or find in the library, or read the Boy Scout or Girl Scout Manual.

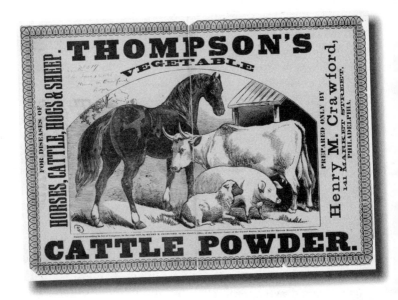

your belly, and now the campfire flames draw filigree patterns against the dark of the night sky. It's time. Let the lying begin. The best stories are told by geezers and codgers, so be sure you have at least one of these individuals in the party. Most of the yarns are based on true happenings.[14] Both the telling and listening are enhanced by occasional swigs from your stash of personal medicinal liquid.[15]

When, finally, you fall into your tent, exhausted but *very* relaxed, you know you'll sleep soundly. Your mistake. An hour later, you awaken. Perhaps you shouldn't have imbibed that gallon of tar-black boiled coffee followed by too many doses of personal medicine. Painfully, you squirm out of your sleeping bag, crawl forth from the tent, and establish yourself on your feet. The number of powder rooms in the forest and on

14 Can be compared to the truthful tales told by fishermen.
15 You don't need a designated driver around a campfire.

the trail are slim to none, so you must avail yourself of "natural" facilities. If you were smart, you pitched your tent near some bushes.

Next morning, early—oh, very—the camp comes to life. You become aware of the smell of bacon frying; you hear horses being led to the river for a drink. Before you try to get up, first feel around for your arms and legs. If you have a pair each attached at the proper location on your torso, go ahead. Rise from your bed. Smell the coffee.

Breakfast begins with platter-sized hotcakes, shingle-thick bacon slices, eggs deep-fried in bacon grease, and more tar-black coffee. You are renewed.[16]

You take Becky to the river for her morning drink, then saddle up. Becky dances a jig in the crisp morning air.

The trail leads across high plains country that stretches to eternity in all directions. The sun beams down, its earlier caressing warmth changing to sauna temperature. You could fry eggs on a rock. You grow increasingly uncomfortable due, once again, to drinking a gallon or so of breakfast coffee. You scan the terrain. Nowhere can you see a tree, not even a small bush. About the time your eyes begin to cross, the trail passes over a dry creek bed where a thin willow struggles for moisture. A contingent of female riders, including you, peels away at a gallop, intending to slake the willow tree's thirst.

Curiously, male persons don't seem to need to "slip away." Occasionally, you note a lone man scout ahead or off to the flank a few yards. He dismounts and stands on the offside of his horse while casting a keen searching eye at the horizon. A few moments of ascertaining there are no lurking hostiles or the odd outlaw, and the fellow mounts up and rejoins the riders.

That night, you camp near an abandoned homestead. A cabin and small attached corral perch tiredly on the edge of a

16   If you're a vegetarian, be advised: Camp cooks do not deal in leeks and lettuce.

draw. Though you mean to stay up with the hardier folk telling exaggerations around the evening campfire, you're beat to a frazzle. Your body crumples. You know you'll sleep well this night. You change into your watermelon-pink bathrobe and drift gratefully into the Land of Nod.

Next morning when you're roused by the noises of horses and voices of riders, you lie there a few seconds to savor moments of half sleep. Usually you skin out of your pink lounger and into jeans and shirt before showing yourself to the world. On this morning, you realize Nature is calling so fiercely you're going to have to take care of that business first. Your flame-pink night garb draws every eye as you emerge from your tent. This is their first sighting of the garment. All are in awe. You can tell by the flying remarks:

"Hey, look, it's Princess Fatima."

"No, it's Big Bird. Big Pink Bird."

"Where's my camera!"

Many memory books now contain a picture of a watermelon-pink–garbed queenly creature framed against a backdrop of prairie, sagebrush, and distant mountains.

You remember the time you rode with the wagon train and followed a piece of the old Bozeman Trail. You're one of thirty outriders.[17] When you pull into rendezvous camp, you count nine covered wagons. Two exactly replicate early prairie schooners. One has its wagon box painted bright early-American blue with wheel rims of brick red and spokes of butter yellow.

A covered wagon is approximately the length of two Cadillacs and half a pickup, end to end. The interiors are so

17 Outriders—that's wagon-train talk for folks who don't have a wagon, but ride alongside on saddle horses.

narrow, two adults seated opposite would rub knees.[18] It's easy to see why the wagons were called prairie schooners; their taut-stretched white canvas tops seem eager to embrace prairie breezes.

You can almost hear the ghosts of those early wagon travelers on the Bozeman Trail, the main route on the way to Oregon. The history of the Trail is saturated with stories of tragedy and bloodshed. William Thomas sought a new life; instead he lost his on the Bozeman Trail. (A true story . . .)

---

18 Possibly this is the reason there were so many babies born along the trail?

The Bloody Bozeman Trail

*John M. Bozeman established a road
on a branch of the Oregon trail,
And settlers traveled along this path,
their dreams like shining grails;
But the way led across the proud-held
land of the fearsome, mighty Sioux,
And the Bozeman Trail was a bloody trail
and the stories it told were true.*

Men ignored the risks, their wives they
kissed, determined they would not fail,
By hundreds and thousands, on rolled the
wagons on the bloody Bozeman Trail.
For this was the trail, the quickest trail,
to Virginia City gold,
Where the nuggets lay like pebbles at play,
some big as a hand could hold.

But it wasn't gold that seized dark
hold of William Thomas's life,
For pneumonia had killed his infant
daughter and Mary, his loving wife;
From anguish and grief he could find
no relief, but William fought his fears,
For Charlie, his son, his only son, was a
lad of just seven years.

William Thomas chose Montana
in the Territory out west,
He meant to join his brother, George;
this move was for the best;
With Charlie, his son, and his friend,
Joe Schultz, William joined a train,
And in his diary he wrote his thoughts
to ease his sorrow and pain.

"I stood by the side of a little lake,
embroidered around with grass,
Its silver surface reflecting the mountains
clear as a looking glass.
I gazed at peaks, at rugged rocks, and
counted the cost and danger,
Cold chills ran through my blood as I
thought upon the adventure."

For a week they traveled with ox-pulled
schooners and a forty-mule wagon train,
And then a government group of a hundred
units joined them on the plains;
The rumbling wagons stretched for
miles under the summer sky,
Heading to Fort Phil Kearney near Sheridan,
Wyoming, where danger was high.

For the Bozeman Trail trespassed across
the hunting grounds of the Sioux,
War party Indians frequently raided,
killing more than a few,

On July twenty-fourth, William Thomas
wrote of a serious Indian attack:
*"Lead wagons drew ahead, but the
ox train stopped three miles back."*

Wagon masters, Kirkendall,
and Dillon and six other men
Rode to the rear where twenty-five
Indians completely surrounded them;
They fought for their lives for several
hours and finally returned to the train,
They carried wagon master Dillon,
mortally wounded, in terrible pain.

At Fort Phil Kearney the wagons halted,
because of threats by the Sioux,
And William Thomas wrote in his
diary the way a poet might do;
He told of the *"brooks of living waters
as gifts of Providence
To parched lips of wearied travelers,"*
his words most reverent.

"For the inexpressible gifts of God,"
he wrote in his leather diary,
*"Are as ice to the fevered brain,
as sleep to the eye that's weary,
As rest to the wearied soul, as the
breast to the restless child.
"Refreshing mercies,"* said William
Thomas, *"in this land so wild."*

And he told of desolate graves of those
the Indians had scalped and slain,
And how *"wild and insatiated wolves"* dug
through the earth like demons insane,
*"With the piteous inmate half uncovered
and the flesh gnawed from his face."*
(William never wrote what young Charlie
thought of this terrifying place.)

His diary reports on beautiful
streams, of valleys of buffalo,
Of grass that reached above his
knees, of deer and antelope.
When breakdowns caused delay,
William fretted at going so slow,
The creeping train continued on
into the country of the Crow.

William Thomas could feel his
future boiling in his bones,
He made a decision to trust in the
Lord and go ahead on his own.
For the next five days, they traveled
alone through country lush and green;
They crossed Clark's Fork of the
Yellowstone and found a pretty spring.

On August twenty-second they forded
the Stillwater, still traveling alone,
And followed the ruts of the Bozeman
Trail down to the Yellowstone.

In his diary he wrote these words:
"Camped for the night a few yards upslope.
Broke out the champagne bottle."
William Thomas had found fresh hope.

On August twenty-third, a band of
twenty Sioux attacked,
William fell with thirteen arrows
piercing his front and back;
Charlie went down with three sharp
arrows assaulting his little body,
The Indians scalped both father and son,
the wounds were fresh and bloody.

A dozen arrows destroyed Joe Schultz,
the Indians scalped him, too.
The warriors plundered the schooner
and ran off William's two prized mules.
A wagon party found the bodies,
the fires still were burning,
They dug a common grave and buried
remains with stomachs churning.

Now, the gravesite's marked by a
highway sign near Greycliff promontory,
William and Charlie Thomas and
Joseph Schultz made history.
They'd nearly reached their long-sought
goal, their future beckoned bright;
But fate and the clash of cultures on the
Bozeman Trail destroyed that right.

John M. Bozeman established a road
on a branch of the Oregon trail,
And settlers traveled along this path,
their dreams like shining grails,
But the way led across the proud-held
land of the fearsome, mighty Sioux,
And the Bozeman Trail was a bloody trail
and the stories it told were true.

THE GREAT MONTANA
CATTLE DRIVE OF 1989

*Wherein you participate in the Great Montana
Cattle Drive of '89, and wherein you pen some
deathless commemorative songs and poems.*

When Montana gets going on a project, look out. They said
it couldn't be done; they said people would get killed; they
laughed a bunch. But when the opportunity floated past your
door to ride in the 1989 Centennial Cattle Drive from Roundup
to Billings, you leaped upon it.

Who participated? 3,337 horses, 2,397 riders, 2,812 cattle,
79 top horse wranglers, and 113 drovers.[19] All fifty-six counties
of Montana were represented, and you're proud to say you
were among 'em. And you survived. So did your horse. The
following is an account of how you fared—all absolutely true.

19 Statistics from the book: *Just Passin' Through* by Marilyn Deacon Pimperton. A
    dandy pictorial and essay account of the drive. You can order a copy from: Country
    Candles Productions, Box 485, Belt, Montana, 59412.

The Great Montana Centennial Cattle Drive Rap

On the Cattle Drive, got some awful sores;
You think I look bad, you should see my horse.
I was duded up, had on western garb;
Wore my pointy-toed boots, you can call me Pard.

Now the next six days, rarely saw those cows;[20]
I was way back there with the social crowd.
On the first night out, camped on cold, hard ground,
I had pounded in stakes, got my tent tied down.

I was settled in when the darned wind blew,
Started eating dust, thick as Mulligan stew.
Then the dad-blamed sky took a turn for worse,
Blew an awful gale, shoulda heard me curse.

I got soaking wet, didn't feel my best,
But the worst thing came when my tent went west.
It went flying high like a kite let loose;
All my clothes went too, fast as poop
through a goose.

When the wagons rolled, the line stretched for miles,
And we trailed 'cross slopes in true Western style.
And reporters sat in a five-seat surrey,
Or they dashed ever'where in a great big hurry.

20 The cattle, herded by the drovers, trailed parallel or ahead of us
outriders—so we couldn't get in the way.

At night circles formed, there were ten in all;
In my Yellow Circle bunch, we sure had a ball.
Afternoons we camped, fed our horses hay,
Got our grubline food, then 'twas time to play.

In the striped tent,[21] pop and beer flowed fast;
There were great loud bands;[22] man, we had a blast.
And the cowboys danced wearing jinglin' spurs,
With their hats throwed back so's to gaze at girls.

As the days went by, didn't bathe at all,
And the dirt caked on, and my skin grew raw.
When the crud built up on my pore ol' hide;
From the doggone smell, you'd a thought I'd died.

So they brought up showers, set 'em on a hill;
When the guys found out, they thought *what a thrill*.
And they sneaked through brush up the hillside there,
Just to watch the girls in lacy underwear.

But the worst times were when I stood in line
At those porta potties, shoulda heard me whine
But inside those potties, the important folks
Did the same drop-job as the plain cowpokes.

21 The Budweiser beer company established giant red-and-white tents
     at each camping spot. At the end of the day, the horses would quicken
     their steps when they spotted the striped tents, and you knew that
     soon you could enjoy a Bud. (Even if you didn't *like* beer, it tasted good
     after a day in the saddle.)
22 Each night in the big tents, there was entertainment: bands, singers,
     dancin', and palaverin'.

But there came a night, we were short of pots;
Looked around and found, the big beer tent had lots.
So a cowboy said, "Gonna git a rope,"
And he threw a loop, drug a pot up-slope.

Then he stopped at camp, got the rope untied;
Only problem was, a guy was still inside.
He was awful scared, he had lost his pants;
Fished him out of there, shoulda seen him prance.

But the greatest fun was around the fire;
We all picked and grinned, never seemed to tire.
As we sang old songs of the Old West ways,
We pretended we lived in olden days.

Wore our duster coats, it was so romantic,
And we told ourselves we were plumb authentic;
We imagined that we were doggone tough,
As we ate our grub, which was catered stuff.[23]

And a preacher married a young lovebird pair
'Mid the dust and the noise in the big tent where
They pledged love and honor in their dusty jeans;
And the crowd clustered 'round thick as jelly beans.

---

23   You signed on to partake of the catered food. You *could* have taken
along your own grub makin's, but you're glad you didn't. At the end of
the day, you were too doggoned tired to have to cook.

But the six-day drive finally reached the end;
On that last day out, rose at four a.m.
They hitched up the wagons, set a snappy pace,
Then the dawn came up, showed its sunshine face.

When we rolled into Billings, all the folks sure waved,
And we felt so proud for our path was paved
With a cheering crowd, we were filled with pride,
For Montana State, her own Cattle Drive.

'Twas Montana folks made the Drive work swell;
As we showed Hollywood it can go to—well . . .
I survived the Drive, now I'm glad I'm home,
And now you must suffer through this
corny damned poem.

To organize all those riders, the ramrodders put people in "circles." Yours was the Yellow Circle. Nights around the campfire were special. Songs, stories, reminiscences, and jokes brought a singular warmth to the evenings. Yours truly wrote a song parody for the Yellow Circle. You may warble to the tune of Yellow Rose of Texas.

Yellow Circle Anthem

We're the Yellow Circle Campfire
On this here Cattle Drive
We're pushin' cows and hopin'
That we will all survive.

We gathered back at Roundup
And camped out on the grass
With horses, cows, and critters
Oh boy, do we have class.

Chorus . . .
And we always will remember
Montana's Cattle Drive
The Eighty-Nine Centennial
If we come out alive.

When we rounded up them dogies
Though folks weren't sure we could
And drove 'em in to Billings
Said, the Hell with Hollywood.

The wagons rolled along behind
Them big old longhorn steers
That kicked up dust and bawled so loud
It liked to bust our ears.
Chorus . . .

And we sang around the campfires
And spent each night in song
And spread our sougans 'neath the stars
Out West where we belong.

The riders came from everywhere
And even overseas
To join Montana's cattle drive,
Take part in history.
Chorus . . .

We showed 'em how it's done Out West,
We opened up our doors
And loaned 'em all our Bag Balm
To salve their saddle sores.

Chorus . . .
And we always will remember
Montana's Cattle Drive
The Eighty-Nine Centennial
If we come out alive.

A CLASSIC STANCE

*Wherein you learn that the facilities
on the open prairie are scanty.*

Whoever originated the philosophy that death and taxes are the only certain events in life has never been on a round-up where the terrain is flat as a floor and bereft of bushes, trees, or any kind of growth taller than a snake's back.

Your friends, Greta and Stuart, volunteer to help gather cattle for a neighboring rancher. It is to be a sizable drive covering more territory than Delaware. Greta, an avid amateur photographer hoping to capture some unusual shots, puts her camera in her saddlebag.

Greta and Stuart, in true western tradition, load their horses into their trailer way before dawn and arrive at the ranch to find the crew already assembled around the breakfast table, enjoying a seventh or eighth or tenth final cup of coffee. For some mysterious reason, probably linked to cowboy hormones, riding for cattle means crawling out of a warm bed in the middle of the night to eat breakfast while it's still pitch dark and then sit around drinking cup after

> Cowboys get up before dawn
> With many a curse and a yawn
> They eat plumb half-hearted
> And wait to get started
> A day they now claim is half gone.

cup of coffee while waiting for daylight so they can see to saddle up.

"Come in and have a bite," say the ranch-owner couple. "It's not daylight yet."[24]

You, Greta, and Stuart sit down to a generous western breakfast of eggs, biscuits, potatoes, pancakes, bacon, and plenty of java.

"More coffee, boys?" says the ranch woman and pours refills all around.

As the sky turns from ink to pink, half a dozen loaded horse trailers pull out and aim toward distant pastures—very distant. The vehicles jostle and bump and bounce over gravel roads and dirt tracks. You and Greta, having frequently found yourselves the only female cowhands amongst a crew of men, are thankful you refused that third cup of coffee.

Arriving at the destination, everybody unloads their horses, mounts up, and commences gathering—often at a fast trot, jig, or lope. As the morning advances, the cowboys began to suffer from coffee overload. It becomes more and more difficult to ignore the mounting pressure. There are no coulees, no gulches, no bushes—only flat, unending prairie pasture.

---

24 You are aware of that; your eyelids are still sleep-glued.

The cowboys, easily embarrassed and too shy to mention personal requirements when in the company of females, continue trotting, loping, jigging, and jogging. The situation might have escalated into possibly serious rupture of important portions of anatomy, but finally one of the crew murmurs something to Stuart and he rides up alongside Greta.

"Hon," says Stuart, "the boys would like you two girls to check for cattle up that draw."

Somewhat mystified, but happy to accommodate, you and Greta ride off. The so-called draw is nothing more than a slight dip about as deep as a saucer but, dutifully, we put our horses over the top. Greta chances a look back. And starts to giggle . . . and chortle.

You follow Greta's gaze and there, skylighted, backs to you two, stands a line of a dozen men in the classic spraddle-legged position.

It is Greta's finest photographic moment.

Part Eight

FROM THE HORSE'S MOUTH

There's many a theory about whether animals have emotions, thoughts, and senses of humor. Whoever tries to tell you a horse doesn't have those qualities, tell that individual to flake off.

CHIEF THE CIRCUS HORSE

Wherein you learn that some horses are their own bosses.

Remember when you were in college? Part of the reason you chose that particular center of higher learning was because its curriculum included horsemanship. Meaning the college kept a stable of horses, and you could elect to take riding courses. Naturally, you signed on to take as many equestrian classes as possible. Not that you needed lessons, since you'd ridden horses since you were two. No, the need lay in the yearning to pet a pony, groom him, smell the tack—all a sure cure for homesickness.

The college equestrian professor tried to keep a stable of gentle horses that wouldn't buck off a greenhorn but at the same time weren't complete dullards. Chief, a small bay, was not a dullard, nor did he ever try to buck. Chief had been a circus horse. He'd let riders do amazing things from his back while he cantered evenly around a ring. That was a plus to you as a college rider. Chief made you look good.

However, the little bay thought he was a person. The circus had taught him an amazing number of tricks, and while

Chief loved everybody, he sometimes got bored if kept in a stall too long. On a slow afternoon, he would unlatch the latch on his pen or slide back the bar on the corral gate and walk the short distance to downtown. He could be on Main Street long before anyone noticed he was missing.

Chief enjoyed visiting stores. Sometimes he'd go into the mercantile and browse the clothing aisles. He particularly enjoyed the saddle shop. The saddle maker liked to fit whatever tack he was making onto Chief to make sure all fitted nicely.

Always a gentleman, Chief never soiled the interior of any building. Town folk tolerated him with amusement and affection. They'd call the school with a message: "Your horse is here again."

Chief was particularly fond of saloons, especially the one in midtown that had an old-fashioned swinging door entryway. Piece of cake for Chief. He'd nose open the door, push on through, and belly up to the bar. The bartender considered him of legal drinking age and would serve him beer in the bottle. Chief knew how to grip the bottle neck with his lips, tilt his head up, and drink 'er down. Then he'd set the empty back on the bar, neat as anything. You could almost hear him sigh with pleasure.

The saloon owner got a kick out of the occasional visit from Chief, but one afternoon the owner wasn't there. Behind the bar stood a stranger—someone who hadn't heard about Chief. When a small bay horse entered the premises, the new bartender said, "Shoo!"

Chief blinked a couple of times and went to his usual spot at the far end of the bar. He waited to be served. The bartender shoved on Chief's shoulder, a useless effort. Chief bobbed his head as if to say, "I'm waiting! I'm thirsty!" Bartender found a piece of rope and looped it around the Chief's neck. He pulled. Chief turned in a circle and let himself be led to the middle of the floor, where he went down on his knees, dropped his rear, and pushed up with his front legs. There he sat, looking like an equine Sphinx.

Bartender shoved, pulled, and shouted to no avail. The poor man was near tears of frustration when the saloon owner stepped through the door. The owner paused.

"Hi, Chief," he said. "Want a beer?"

Chief bobbed his head and whuffled, "Yes."

The new bartender fainted.

Horsing Around

ITTY BITTY HORSES

*Wherein you learn that a pony is a pony,
but a miniature horse is a horse.*

You own miniature horses and you're often razzed about this sad affliction, especially if you live in working ranch or farm country where minis are considered a joke. Someone even wrote an exceedingly short poem on the question of miniature horses.

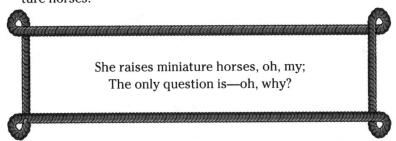

She raises miniature horses, oh, my;
The only question is—oh, why?

There's an answer to that facetious ditty. Yesterday, while feeding hay to five minis enclosed in a corral, a bale string attacked. It leaped off the ground and snaked around your foot.

The question might be asked: Why was a bale string lurking on the ground anyway? You should be ashamed. Everybody knows it's against the code of the true horse person to allow baling twine to roam freely on the range or in the corral. Anyone knows that bale strings must be gathered together, tied in bundles, and placed in the bed of the pickup where they ride around till spring. Or some folks prefer hanging the twine on upright poles stuck in the pole-holes of the pickup where they wave like a comet's tail 'til the first tulips bloom. Still others drop the twine clumps in the burn barrel and when the barrel is full, the contents are set on fire.[1]

Whatever disposal style is used, the point is this—it's a big sin to have strings littering the terrain. So, why was a rogue bale string loitering in your corral? Why hadn't you captured and incarcerated it along with fellow strings?

Weather is the answer. The string somehow went unnoticed among the horse apples. One end of the twine sank its tail deeply into the mire and froze there, resisting all your efforts to pull it out.

No problem, you thought. A warm day would come along, then you'd yank the orange cord loose. That was your mistake.

While you weren't paying attention, the evil twine formed a loop and you learned just how a calf feels in a team-roping contest. That string caught you by the heel and you went kersplat—facedown in the plentiful pile of horse apples. Said apples cushioned your fall, but were less than tasty.[2]

You are lying flat in the middle of a space where there is no handy snubbing post, ledge, or other solid gear to use to hoist yourself upright. This might become a problem, unless you're young and agile, in which case you can rise as fast as a

---

1 Best to keep bags of marshmallows in the pantry. Visiting children can be sent out to roast marshmallows while the adults palaver in the kitchen.
2 Don't try to make cider from horse apples.

bouncing rubber ball. If, however, you suffer from a busted leg or other debilitating condition such as being older than dirt, your lower extremities either don't work properly or have the springiness and strength of cooked noodles. You lie there, contemplating the world from a worm's-eye view.

Meanwhile, five miniature horses are busily munching on the hay you've spread. One of them, a filly curious as a cat, wanders over and puts her nose down to yours. In horse language, she says, "Whatcha doin'?"

"Trying to get up," you reply.

The filly begins nuzzling your pocket where she is sure you are hiding a horse-cake treat.

"Go away," you growl, as you struggle to establish your feet under you. Nothing works. You need a handhold on something vertical in order to winch up. You grab the filly's front leg, then reach for her mane. She lifts her head and you hang on while she indignantly backs away. You manage to slide both arms around her neck. She speeds up her backward velocity.

The filly became your hairy handhold, a furry anchor, a hirsute helper. She is the reason you are able to establish a vertical view of the world. Once upright and in charge of your limbs, you whip out your pocketknife[3] and cut the killer bale string off at its roots. Gratefully you then reward your assisted-living filly a sweet treat, return to the house, shed your horse-apple-coated garments, and indulge in a nice, hot, apple-removing shower.

And that, oh poet, is why you have miniature horses.

---

3 You cannot be a true horse person unless you carry a pocketknife. Swiss Army is considered de rigueur.

LANDSCAPE ART

Wherein you learn a different style of horse-catching.

As a horse aficionado, you may be of the skeptical persuasion and thus view the following as a made-up story. You'd be wrong. The main event is absolutely true. The names of people, animals, and small towns are manufactured.

On an otherwise normal day, your friend Ophelia says, "Your birthday? I have the perfect gift for you."

"Oh?" you respond, ever alert when someone uses your name in the same sentence as the word "gift."

"Yes," says Ophelia. "I'm going to give you Tinker Belle." Ophelia's grin grows broader. "I have too many miniatures, and I know the little filly will have a good home with you. She's just a year old."

Which is how you come to be pulling a horse trailer down the interstate to the small town of Belly Button, Montana. You've drafted another friend, Lulubelle, to ride shotgun and act as navigator and assistant horse loader. Lulubelle, studying the directions you'd obtained, instructs, "Keep going straight through Belly Button, continue on for two miles, then turn left at Dead Skunk Road. Another mile, then make the hairpin turn, go another half mile, you'll come to a Y. Take the left fork up the hill and continue to the second green double-panel gate."

Piece of cake. The day is cloudy, the temperature nippy, but no wind. We reach Ophelia's establishment and trundle through the gate and onward to a large, metal, barnlike structure set at the edge of a pasture about the size of Delaware. Out in the field eight or ten Lilliputian horses and three normal-size equines gambol about.

You pull up by the barn and you and Lulubelle debark from the pickup. Ophelia appears. We three humans scrunch over and slip beneath a two-wire electric fence into the pasture, then walk around to the rear of the metal building. You cannot discern any pens, corral, or entry doors into the building. How, you wonder, will Ophelia corral the herd if there's no holding area?[4] There is, however, a very large rubber tub into which Ophelia pours half a bag of sweet feed. She whistles. The miniatures sashay close and begin munching on feed. You and Lulubelle remain quiet, trying not to spook any critter.

"Need this?" you suggest, holding out the halter that you're carrying.

"No, I'll just grab her," says Ophelia. "I'll slip up behind and throw my arms around her neck. When I do that," she adds, "you two come up on the other side."

"Huh?" says Lulubelle, a first-rate horsewoman. She raises her eyebrows in surprise.[5]

Little Tinker Belle is elusive, refusing to stand in one place long enough for Ophelia to drift up behind her. The little horse dances around the perimeter of the sweet-feed tub. Ophelia and Tinker Belle do a ballet dance until at last Tinker Belle is

4   You optimistically assume the horses are easy to catch. Optimism can sometimes be a detrimental attitude.
5   For the first time in her life, Lulubelle is speechless.

positioned in between two other minis—all with their heads down, slurping up feed from the tub. Ophelia eases up to Tinker Belle's southern aspect, then launches herself onto the kneecap-high miniature filly. Both minis on either side of Tinker explode like popcorn on a hot skillet while Tinker Belle, having four feet to work with, takes flight with Ophelia attached. With her chore coat flapping, Ophelia looks much like a large fruit bat as Tinker drags her across rough, half-frozen ground.

"Come up, come up!" shouts Ophelia. Lulubelle, holding a halter, steps forward but by then, Ophelia is forced to let go of the filly or have all the flesh on her knees torn from the bone.

"You should have grabbed her on the other side," Ophelia admonishes Lulubelle.

"Oh," says Lulubelle, "I guess I didn't understand your horse-catching technique."

Meanwhile, you remain standing by, observing the entertainment.[6]

The entire herd of equines has scattered to the far end of the pasture. It's a nice day for a hike, which is what the three of you do as you trudge on shank's mare to shepherd the bunch back toward the barn. Once again, the horses go to the trough for feed.[7] Once again, Ophelia fails to hang on to Tinker.

Suffice it to say, Tinker Belle does not get caught, but she and Ophelia get a lot of exercise. Ophelia, both knees scraped, finally gives up.

Tentatively you suggest, "Instead of tackling, wouldn't it be easier to halter-break the filly? Or build a small holding corral?"

"Oh," says Ophelia, "I don't do any of that. In fact, I don't do anything with my horses. I just like to watch them. I call them 'Landscape Art.'"

---

6 You have decided that tackling a horse, even a little bitty one, is not your forte.
7 Apparently this is a game with them. They don't seem excited or fearful.

IT TAKES A BANGTAIL
TO BRING IN THE HERD

*Wherein you learn that a good cow horse
is the hardest-working hand on the ranch.*

This is a true story. In the thirties, wild horses overran the range, and the government hired riders to capture them. A rancher might run in a bunch of wild horses, then turn over half a dozen each to however many kids he had, with instructions to "ride 'em."

Bobby Kramer was one of the old-time cowgirls featured in the documentary *I'll Ride That Horse!* still available at Montana State University. The documentary interviewed women rodeo riders of the times: Bobby Kramer, the Brander sisters, the Greenough sisters, and others. Bobby continued to ranch and raise "flying red horses" well into her eighties.

Wild Horse Catcher

Few remember when loose horses
roamed, galloping wild and free;
When thundering hooves raised billows of
dust as far as eyes could see.

Bobby Kramer has ridden those trails,
she opens memory's door
To tell of broncs and horses roped,
stories by the score.

"We gathered wild horses out of the
badlands; chased 'em out of hills,
And broke 'em rough and saddled 'em
up and rodeo'd for the thrills.

"Nowadays, most horses are tame, the
wild ones cleared from the range;
Savin' the grass for cattle; ain't no
way to hold back change.

"My husband and me, we needed the
money right after World War II,
So we hired on as crew to round
'em up. And we did—all but a few.

"This one cagey bunch got away from
us all, led by a pinto mare.
She dodged our ropes, broke through
traps, no fence could hold her there.

"That mare, descended from thoroughbreds,
    you couldn't catch or check.
You know that place where the land goes
    on from Haxby's point to Fort Peck?

"You know that place where the Missouri
    River comes in there on one side?
And the Little Dry and Big Timber Creeks
    join up like a double tide?

"It was there the ranchers built corrals
    to force them horses to pause;
We used an airplane, flew over the herd,
    spooked 'em out of the draws.

"But the riders below were too far back,
    the bunch just swarmed round the end,
There wasn't no turn in that pinto mare,
    she drove right through them men.

"The ranchers they bet the wily pinto
    would never be taken alive;
Regardless of riders or blind corrals,
    somehow that mare would contrive

"To pound on through and scatter the bunch and
    head for the badlands to hide.
There wasn't no turnin' that pinto mare.
    No turnin'. God knows we tried.

"She'd always take off on a partic'lar
trail headin' for the Badlands,
Then back she'd come, down to the
point, leading the whole darned band.

"Now Fort Peck Lake is deep, with
many a narrow tributary
Extending like claws into the draws,
lurking to trap the unwary.

"Hitting a stream, the bunch would swim
to reach the other shore—
All but that pinto mare. She'd swerve
and take to the breaks once more.

"So, then my husband said, 'Bobby,
you think you could rope that mare?'
'Well, I can give it a try,' I told him,
taking it as a dare.

"I flew my plane to pester the mare to go
toward the point of land,
Then set down my Cessna and got on
my horse, just the way I'd planned.

"I took my rope and tied through the
fork, tied it hard and fast.
Then, cinching up tight, I rode to cut
trail before that mare got past.

"Now, rain had soaked the ground to
gumbo, slowing my saddle horse,
But soggy earth slowed the mare as well
as she fled on her headlong course.

"I drew in close and threw my loop at
that weaving, bobbing head;
For a second I thought my rope was too
short and I watched it sail with dread.

"But the lariat settled like a necklace
around that pinto's surging neck,
And I set back, jerked up my slack,
and knew the mare was checked.

"My husband, he saw the struggle, but
he was across on the other side.
That mare was crazy mad; no rope
had ever touched her hide.

"When she'd hit the end of my string
and found she couldn't get away,
She'd squeal, back up, and try to kick me,
determined to make me pay.

"But I had her charged to my saddle
horn and unless that rope it broke,
I wasn't about to let her go.
I pulled a tighter choke.

"My husband, he come ridin' up,
    aiming to help me out.
I surely was glad to see him there;
    that mare was mighty stout.

"We threw her down a number of
    times; the mare just wouldn't quit.
We'd let her up, but she'd go wild
    and fling another fit.

"We got her in the corral, cross-hobbled
    to keep her from jumpin' out.
My husband was grinnin' and I sure
    knew what proud was all about.

"Though we gave her a home, her spirit
    was gone, as if she didn't care.
At times, I've wished I'd let her go,
    that free-running pinto mare.

"But no matter what happens, no matter
    what burden I'm ever called to bear,
I can look back and remember the thrill—
    when I roped that pinto mare."

COUNTRY COUSIN, CITY COUSIN

*Wherein you communicate with City Cousin
about your "boring" country life.*

Dear City Cousin,

You wanted to know how things are going with me. Pretty much the same old same old. Today started with my young mare stealing the keys from my mechanical mule.[8] She has a bad habit of using her mouth to untie ropes, open gates, pull buckets out of truck beds, and generally get into trouble. She nibbled the keys right out of the ignition and dropped them in the snow. Which meant I couldn't drive the four-wheeler to do chores, which meant things got a little behinder.

I needed to go into town to the feed store, but Jake, the puppy, swiped my spectacles and refused to tell me where he hid them. I dug out an old, outdated pair that gives me fierce headaches, but does allow me to distinguish road signs, street signs, and small children when I'm driving.

8   Not a metal robot on stilts.

In town, I parked in front of the feed store and accidentally locked both truck doors. The right door has a problem. Once locked, if I try to use a key to open it from the outside, the key hangs up like a goose egg in a snake's throat. I couldn't get the danged thing out or turn it. Being Girl Scout trained and all, I always carry a spare key in my purse. Unfortunately, said pocketbook was stashed behind the seat inside the locked truck.

Using the above-mentioned Girl Scout ingenuity, I went to the back and opened up the door of the truck's camper-shell, unloaded two blocks of salt, moved aside a sack of grain, a box of books, the trailer hitch, a pair of four-buckles, a bucket of ropes and halters, and a sheep hook. I crawled in, my knees screaming in protest, and shoved open the sliding glass window of the shell, but somebody had latched the *truck's* sliding window from the inside. I could have been at a loss, but my quick Girl Scout mind seized on another plan. Utilizing the sheep hook, my Swiss Army knife, and my temper, which had become seriously tested, I bashed the latch till it popped, sheep-hooked the purse from behind the seat, and drew it forth like a world-class fly-fisher-person. My form was flawless; crowds—had there been any—would have cheered.

In the feed store I paid for my purchases and then departed for home. The telephone rang as I entered my front door. It seems I'd forgotten my pocketbook at the feed store, so now I have to go back to town. While there, I may as well visit the eye doctor to order a new pair of specs, as my regular ones are still missing, but the good news is: a chinook melted the snow some and I've found the keys to my mule.

Hope all goes well with you in the city,
      Your Country Cousin

HORSETALK

Wherein you learn that horses
have their own language.

They're at it again. A group of a dozen or so horses are pastured for the winter on acreage bordering your south fence. These are working saddle horses who earn their keep carrying dude-ranch guests during the summer and laze about all winter gossiping. On this side of the fence, your own six bangtails form a welcoming committee.

Daily the equines chit-chat across the fence. They gather on a regular basis to exchange news, to engage in general horse chatter, and to complain about their owners. It's like a lodge meeting or an after-church social hour. South of the fence, there's Shorty, Blaze, Graybear, Brownie, Dandy, Blackie, Big Bay, and several others who hang back, too shy to be introduced. Big Bay seems to be the club's president.

Your two mares, Becky and Pretty Girl; three geldings, Cherokee, Cochise, and Cheyenne; and the filly, Cinnamon, stand in a row facing the crowd on the other side of the fence. Becky is group leader for this side. The conversation goes something like this:

Big Bay: "Well, here we are again, down from the hills for the winter."

Becky: "I see that. So, how was your summer?"

Big Bay: "Oh, so-so. I went out every couple of days carrying a dude along mountain trails. Pretty boring, usually."

Becky: "Boring? At least you got to see some different country. I've been stuck here on this measly pasture all summer. I got out only once when a wagon train rolled through. Traveled with it for a couple of miles carrying my mistress. The woman needs to lose weight. She's not as young as she used to be and neither am I. Take a look at my back. Notice how it sags?"

Big Bay: "Looks all right to me. At least you're short. If you were as tall as I am, and a dude horse, you'd have to carry really heavy weights. Why, there was one tubby guest who could have been a sumo wrestler. I tried to get out of that job, I tell you. Tried to pretend I was lame, but the wrangler wouldn't buy it. He just slapped an extra-large saddle on me and drug over a stepstool so this sorry fat guy could climb aboard."

Pretty Girl: "I've worn a saddle a couple of times. It's not too bad."

Cherokee: "I haven't. What's it like?"

Becky: "Shut up, twerps. I'll let you know when you can speak."

Big Bay: "As I was saying, life as a dude horse has its drawbacks. Now, the wranglers have put us dude horses on this dryland pasture for the winter. I'll probably be skin and bones by spring."

Becky: "I know what you mean. Grass is tasteless this time of year."

Big Bay: "I see your mistress tosses out flakes of hay to you. And every day at that! Sure wish you'd share."

Becky: "I can tell. You've about broke the fence down trying to reach over."

Big Bay: "Well, that hay just looks delicious. And you and your group are all too tubby anyway."

Becky: "Oh, is that right?!" She bit Big Bay on the nose, turned toward Cherokee and Pretty Girl and ordered, "Come on group, back to the corral. It's time for our mistress to show up to feed us. But she'll probably be late. She usually is. She ought to be fired."

Big Bay: (calling out) "See you tomorrow?"

Becky: (over her shoulder) "Maybe."

Horsing Around

HORSEMANSHIP 101

*Wherein you learn that attending a horse clinic is
an affair to remember, and wherein a chiropractor
becomes your new best friend.*

You might have followed the south end of cattle for miles or ridden the mountain trails for days or participated in a jillion horseback events, but you're lousy as a horse trainer. You're way too soft in the heart (and possibly the head) to train a green horse, so every so often you sign on to participate in a horse "clinic."[9] This one happens to be a "colt clinic."

You load up your two-year-old filly who is as gentle as the proverbial kitten, but a lot bigger. Her name is Jolly, and she fits her name. She's halter broke and you've even been on her a time or two. You're sure the clinic will turn her into a fine-tuned steed.

The professional trainer accepts no more than ten riders. He feels he can give each one personal attention if he keeps the enrollment limited. You feel fortunate to be included—a lone female person amid a field of nine males, plus the trainer.

---

9   Clinic does not refer to illness in horse or you . . . at least at first.

The class is held in a local covered arena and begins with all ten colts haltered and grouped inside a portable metal corral about the size of a large broom closet. You and the other humans are on foot, hanging on to your horse's halter lead rope. You are instructed to mount up—*one at a time* under the watchful eye of the trainer.[10] Because you're the only woman in the class, Trainer gallantly invites you to go first. You climb aboard Jolly. You are not, however, allowed to keep the lead rope in your hands. No, the trainer holds it. He explains why.[11]

The other nine classmates watch politely except for one macho know-it-all. He disdains any wussy waiting and swings aboard his mount—a big, five-year-old, never-been-ridden sorrel mare he calls Masie. Macho Man hits the saddle and Masie Mare blows up. She drops her nose, snorts, and erupts into a bucking frenzy. Jolly, your own little filly (upon whom you are seated with nothing but air to hang onto) panics. She pitches. You happen to be crowded next to the metal sides of the corral, so you make a swan-dive reach for the top rail. Your face rattles down the metal bars like a stick along a picket fence. Thankfully, the earth, when you smack into it, is rock free.[12]

The trainer retrieves your fallen self and catches your filly.[13] He then instructs you to remount, which you do.[14] Next he leads you *out* of the enclosure and stations you alongside. You still have no lead rope in your hands. Does Sir Trainer hand it to you? No, he hands it to one of the watchers, of which there is a small crowd. Apparently, taking all control away from the rider is some new technique, which you don't question.[15]

10   Watch out for watchful eyes. They could bode trouble.
11   Explanation makes no sense.
12   It is not a soft landing.
13   Macho Man is also on the ground, but in true manly fashion gets up all by himself.
14   Unless both legs are broken or you've put out an eye, you always get back on.
15   Boy, are you dumb.

Two minutes pass by. Within the corral-pen, Masie Mare blows up once again. Startled, the helpful individual holding your filly's lead rope throws up her hands, spooking the already frightened Jolly who commences bucking across the landscape. For two jumps you stay with her, then you choose to soar gracefully to earth.[16]

For the next week at the coffee shop in town where the good ol' boys gather to gossip, the favorite topic is all about watching you go off your horse.

It's a long while before you attend another clinic. But time heals. To a different trainer you take Music, a green-broke mare who has never tried to buck. You've ridden her some and feel confident that you'll both benefit from the experience.

This trainer holds his clinic in the middle of a large pasture. The weather is raw and windy with low, gray clouds scudding across the sky. Mr. Trainer wears a microphone headset through which he shouts instructions to a class of thirty-two riders. Personal attention is not this trainer's particular forte. In fact, he sounds a tinge testy, as if he prefers dealing with horses only and wishes their riders would go home.

Through the microphone he describes a "one-rein" stop. This means that should you be in a tight situation, say, the side of a steep hill, or your horse is trying to take the bit and run, you, the skilled horse-person, should pull your pony's head around with one rein, causing cessation of your steed's forward movement.

Trainer makes the class practice. "One-rein stop!" he shouts. He adds caustic observations on various pupils' performances.

16   It's the quick-stop landing that hurts.

Since you have a habit of striving to please,[17] you pull the rein and pull the rein. Music, the mare, bends her head and bends. She doesn't, however, move her feet. She keeps on "bending" till she loses her balance and falls over sideways, thumping the ground like a dropped rock. You're still in the saddle, your near leg under her. Music scrambles to her feet, then stands gazing down at you, a surprised expression in her eyes. You remain on your back, viewing the heavens.

Trainer Man dashes over. He squats by your side. He looks both worried and irritated. Another rider hovers over you. "I'm a doctor," she says. "Are you hurt? Your leg? Is it hurt?"

You have become the center of attention. From your supine, worm's-eye perspective, you are being peered at by a ring of persons staring downward. You glare up at the throng and reply with a word that rhymes with "slit."

Naturally, you get back on. While no bones are broken, your dignity is seriously dented, plus your neck bones seem to have changed places. Your back vertebrae ditto, but getting back in the saddle is a must. However, your parts have seized up. Music is a tall mare. You fail to lift your left foot into the stirrup. Casting a desperate eye about,[18] you spot a pickup drawn up like a bleacher. The endgate is down and seated thereon are four audience members. Leading Music, you stumble to the vehicle. The watchers roll out of the way. You squirm, belly down, onto the endgate, grab the pickup sides and struggle to your knees, then crank to your feet. You are not a pretty sight. But from your elevated position, you can now step across into the saddle.

Tomorrow you'll be visiting your new best friend, the chiropractor.

---

17 Are there support groups available to those suffering from the striving-to-please syndrome? Please advise.

18 A desperate eye looks a little like a marble aggie.

From the Horse's Mouth

I've been rode by heaps o' cowboys,
Some short, some fat, some tall.
Some kind, some mean, some green,
And some I can't recall.

But cowpokes always think they know
What makes a top cow horse.
Them fellers poke and prod and pat
And knowingly discourse.

They speculate about my age
By looking at my teeth,
And check for bone and eye and brain
And how I am beneath.

They want a mount of easy gait
That's wide between the eyes,
And high in withers, deep in chest
Well-muscled is a prize.

If I could talk, I would complain
Cuz cowboys sure are strange.
I've been rode in heat, in cold, in rain
And snows out on the range.

When mornin' light has barely showed,
A son-of-a-gun appears;
He's got hisself a hankerin'
To round up some ol' steers.

Before I've finished out my sleep,
This bow-legged feller gits me;
I ain't had my breakfast yet,
With oats he plans to trick me.

But that don't fool this old horse,
I turn my tail and run.
It ain't no use, he gits a rope
Which ruins all my fun.

The corral I circle tryin' to hide,
But the sizzling lasso falls.
With crow-hopping quiver, I halt in my tracks.
"I gottcha," the cowpoke drawls.

He slips a halter on my nose
And ties me to a post.
And then that Drink-of-Water goes
(And this I hate the most)—

To fetch a funny leather thing
Of metal, straps, and chain.
He pats me nice and friendly like,
I know I'm in for pain.

"Go easy, Pard," the cowboy says,
And shoves it on my face;
The bit he pokes between my teeth,
And pulls my ears in place.

He buckles up the throat-latch snug,
And though I settle down,
I will keep my options open wide
With this here cowpoke clown.

He spreads a blanket on my back,
It gives my hide the itch
Where sweat from former rides has caked.
Sure wish he'd wash the son-of-a . . . gun.

And when I look around again,
He's coming with a hunk
Of leather-covered knobs and swells,
I know that I am sunk.

With lift of arm and mighty swing,
He slaps the saddle on;
I hump my back, but it's no use,
My dignity has gone.

And then he grabs the latigo,
Draws up the cruel cinch;
And though I swell up like a blimp,
Of slack there's not an inch.

And when I'm dressed in heavy leather,
The cowboy piles aboard;
We travel prairie, plain and draw,
(I'm better than a Ford).

But though it ain't the easy life,
It's still the one for me,
Cuz, I'm a workin' cow horse. Please,
Don't put no dudes on me!

Part Nine

HORSE HEAVEN

There is no end, no bottom, no final story if you're a horse lover. Some stories are humorous, some are nostalgic, and many can be tragic. Life with your horse (or mule if you're into extra-long ears) is a blessing for which you can't give enough thanks.

Horsing Around

37

HORSE WRECKS AND HORSE SENSE

Betty Lynne's story . . .

Betty Lynne Grue McCarthy grew up on an eastern Montana ranch. She rides and ropes with the best. She and her husband run cattle, sheep, and goats on their spread. This is her story, in her words.

October is a tricky time in eastern Montana. A solid freeze every night, a good thaw by 10 a.m. This combination leaves a horse's footing on the clay banks along coulees less than good.

I only had to trail one cow with a younger calf down to the next pasture, just about half a mile. She was reluctant to leave, but I was riding a four-year-old Morgan cross named Bay who was really taking to the business of watching a cow. Bay has been my biggest challenge to train. Not one to buck, if he could spook and enjoy a good run-away first. But we'd reached somewhat of an agreement, and he was getting more "cowy"[1] at every saddling.

1   Cowy: Savvy about how to trail, herd, and gather cattle.

I was still uneasy about giving Bay his head, though, especially on a slippery fall morning. But when the cow changed her mind about traveling south, ducked off into a draw, and headed back, I hurried along the top to get ahead of her, then started down the bank to head her off.

I felt Bay's front feet slide out from under him but thought he could catch himself. So I stayed with him. A bad decision. When his shoulder hit the mud, it was too late.

I kicked loose from the saddle and started scrambling, but I had nowhere to go but downhill. I could hear Bay rolling over and over behind me, unable to catch himself. I thought I was finally clear and looked back over my shoulder only to see Bay still right with me on our muddy descent—now all four legs in the air. His bulk settled over and came to rest across my legs. I don't know why I couldn't get away from him; he appeared to be rolling in slow motion.

Now, I lay plastered in the mud, looking at the underside of my cinches and the belly of a very touchy four-year-old colt—one who has stampeded from me when I merely crinkled up a gum wrapper. His front hooves were inches from my head, back hooves closer still. I knew he was going to try to spring to his feet in a moment, and I knew that his trying would thrash me to oblivion.

I could reach his right shoulder, and I started talking low and petting him, hoping he wouldn't panic. I knew I was up against instinct and nature for him not to try getting to his feet. He started to stir and kick and raised his head far enough to see me under him. I figured I was as good as dead, but he wilted. His legs relaxed, and his head dropped back to the ground.

I kept talking to him, rubbing his shoulder, but now I was afraid to wiggle for fear it would set him off. So, there we lay in the warm October sun.

Finally, I gathered the nerve to try to pull myself free. Nothing. Couldn't budge. Tried harder. Still nothing. So far, Bay

Colt lay still as stone. Finally, a light came on and I unbuckled my chaps belt. They were a pair of warm winter shotguns that fully encased my legs. By pushing against the cinch (I wasn't going to shove on his belly!), I gained an inch. Then another. I felt something pull loose in one knee, but I had to keep trying. Finally, I popped free and stood in my stocking feet in the frozen mud.

Bay scrambled to his feet, leaving hoofprints across my flattened chaps and boots, still pressed in the mud.

So I sobbed awhile and hugged Bay Colt's neck, then got redressed and went after that cow and calf. They had returned to the same spot we'd started from.

I was left with a bad limp and a new knowledge. I learned that it's the grace of God and these magnificent animals that allow me to share their lives.

And I learned that no cow can ever completely get away. This continent is surrounded by oceans. I'll catch up to her eventually!

BUSTED UP

*Wherein you learn that hospitals are
often familiar places to mule riders.*

Hospital emergency rooms in rural western towns are familiar places to anyone who uses horses in his/her daily work—such as cowboys and cowgirls. Usually, a wounded rider—wounded due to being involved as a main participant in a horse or mule wreck (though berserk bulls are sometimes responsible)—is hauled to the hospital. There the doctors and medical staff do their best to keep the cowboy from leaving before he stops bleeding.[2]

Sandy Seaton Sallee grew up in Yellowstone National Park, where she rode horses among the elk and drove four-up stagecoaches. Today, she co-owns Black Mountain Outfitters with her husband, Scott, and is a cowgirl poet who has been featured at the National Cowboy Poetry Gathering in Elko, Nevada. Her poem, "Alone," details the terrible wreck Scott had while riding for cattle in the high country on a green mule.

2   Or the busted bones are set.

Alone

Did I feel a jolt of anguish?
Lord, how could I not?
Scott was comatose, alone
Mule leaving at a trot . . .

I was whistling in our pasture
Catching our buckskin colt
I was smiling in the sunshine
When his mule began to bolt.

Scott was dragging in the stirrup
Dirt dancing off his head
I was brushing off the gelding
Never felt the awful dread.

But shouldn't I have known it?
He's my partner and my friend
Our two lives beat together
As one heart without end.

He's sorting pairs to move them east
An old cow hid in brush
Scott went to move her day-old calf
She hit him in a rush.

Scott's unconscious. Body breaking
That Angus cow was hot
Knocked them through the five wire gate
The big mule smashing Scott.

He would remember two long strides
Then nothing in the black
The mule panicked and she bolted
She galloped through the slack.

Scott bounced off river rocking
He drug through cottonwood
Another rider far away
Saw the mule and understood.

But Scott was nowhere near her
The rider called his name
The day was filled with lonesome
This dread he couldn't tame.

Look! A cow is watching closely
A pile of river rock
The rider follows bovine's gaze
Scott gasps but cannot talk.

His back divided by the break
His ribs are cracked in two
His lungs and liver bleeding hard
His lips are turning blue.

Scott travels worlds far away
He thinks he sees his dad
His head is floating in the sky
He's shivering and sad.

But waking up to God's green earth
The sunshine burns his eyes
His head is throbbing in his skull
A curlew softly cries.

His hair is jerked right from the roots
He's bleeding from the tug
But he won't ever know the wreck
Or remember being drug.

Scott slept there by the Yellowstone
On ancient stone and land
He fought his way back to my heart
This man that wears our brand.

It scares me that I didn't know
That half of me was torn
I touch his face and feel his warmth
I feel we've been reborn.

I know hands who've lost someone
They cowboy up—they try
I almost knew their roar of pain
Thank God Scott didn't die.

THE MAGIC HORSE

Deborah's story . . .

Deborah Collins ranches with her husband in Oklahoma. A transplant from England, Deborah has an abiding love for horses. She generously shares this story of one of her favorite steeds.

My first introduction to Clyde was when I stood looking at a pair of feathered heels, a tail that swished with cussedness, and ears that laid back listening to my every move. I intended to halter him, but he stood, head facing into the corner of the field. Even with hobbles on, front to back, he had somehow managed to escape from his own pasture. Black as midnight, he wore a perfect white star in the middle of his forehead.

Somehow I knew he was all bluff; I just had to wait him out. After about half an hour he turned his head to look at me. Finally, he turned toward me and, quietly, I walked to him and slipped the halter over his nose and soft, pricked ears.

Clyde taught me so much. He deepened my love for horses. Because he was hard mouthed, I rode him in a hackamore. One evening, it took me an hour and a half to catch him. Once he gave in, I saddled up and experienced a beautiful moonlight ride I will never forget.

I was told that Clyde had a "bad eye" and would pull back when tied. He never did. As his character unfolded, my love for him grew and ultimately he learned to trust me.

Clyde formed a close bond with Mary, an old mare. I saw teamwork and affection between the pair that I never would have believed had I not seen it with my own eyes. One morning I walked out to the pasture to catch Clyde. The sun was just rising, and hard, white frost sparkled upon every blade of grass. He'd been lying down next to the mare, but he got to his feet as soon as he heard the gate open. Dragon breath gently plumed from his velvet nostrils and frost-iced whiskers. Old Mary stayed lying down. Before I reached Clyde, he began nosing Old Mary, gently nudging her withers, whickering softly. I stood still, watching.

Clyde positioned himself directly in front of Old Mary and waited. With obvious discomfort, the mare unfolded her long front legs until they were straight out before her. Clyde then reached forward and bit Mary about halfway down her mane. Bracing his front legs for leverage he pulled back. As he tugged, the mare stiffened her front legs and pushed with her back legs. Between Clyde pulling and Old Mary pushing, the mare got to her feet.

Once she was standing, Old Mary shook her neck while Clyde stood by. Then, stepping forward, Old Mary began rubbing and nibbling Clyde along his neck. Clyde exchanged the favor and the pair pampered each other with mutual grooming.

It was like watching an old married couple's morning ritual, a ritual forged with love and by necessity. Though we are taught that horses don't experience emotions as humans do, I believe they come close.

My love for the magical animal called *horse* has shaped my life into what it is today.

Horsing Around

40

THE END OF THE TRAIL

Wherein the days dwindle down . . .

Take care of your horse and your horse will take care of you. The pleasure doesn't stop. As you travel the trail to that final dawn, you may arrive at a time when you can't make your aging body climb into the saddle, but you can still *lean* on Dobbin or Blaze or Dusty or Star.

You can brush their coats, spoil them with carrots and mints, and greet them when they wander up to the house from the pasture (where they linger in the carport, leaving horse dumplings where they hadn't oughta).

If people ask, "What do you *do* with your horses," tell them: "It's not what I do with them, it's what they do with me." Or perhaps mention that you intend to keep them until you can no longer lift a hayfork or a curry comb. Or you can sweetly inform the questioner that when you croak, you've willed your horses to him/her. Or make up any kind of story. Who's going to prove something different? Or you can merely smile and pretend you've gone deaf and didn't hear the question. Sooner or later, the Nosy Parker Person will drop the subject.

Cloud Ponies

Horses, horses, horses, you see
through that old window pane,
Horses, horses, horses that help me
through life's weary game;
I can endure, even smile, as you surely can see,
For when I'm in the saddle on my horse,
I am truly free.

Riding, riding, riding, riding in the sky,
Riding, riding, riding my cloud pony and I.

Crossing the prairie, on the back
of my old buckskin mare,
When she carries me I am free from every care;
Quarter horse, Morgan, or Arab or fine Appaloose,
Tennessee Walker or just ordinary common cayuse.

Riding, riding, riding, riding in the sky,
Riding, riding, riding my cloud pony and I.

Trailing the wind, I will gather my long-ago dreams,
On the back of my horse I know
what true freedom means;
When age sinks its claws and my
body starts to slow down,
When I can't reach the stirrups so
very high off of the ground.

Horses, horses, horses, my old partner—my friend,
Horses, horses, horses, I'll ride as I wait for the end;
After my death if the gods will please ride by my side,
I'll saddle cloud ponies; across heaven forever I'll ride.

Riding, riding, riding, riding in the sky,
Riding, riding, riding my cloud pony and I.

About the Author

For more than forty years, Gwen Petersen has been a rancher and writer of the western persuasion. A cowboy/cowgirl/ranch-woman poet, Gwen was featured at the inaugural National Cowboy Poetry Gathering in Elko, Nevada, established the first Montana Cowboy Poetry Gathering, and appeared on Johnny Carson's *The Tonight Show,* which still surprises her.

Today, this Erma Bombeck of the barnyard writes and directs the annual Toot, Snoot, 'n Hoot Whippin' and Spurrin' Comedy Show. She is the author of numerous books, including the celebrated *How to Shovel Manure,* a hilarious look at country life, *The Greenhorn's Guide to the Woolly West*, and *The Whole Shebang.* Her other writings include short stories, articles, plays, skits, and the syndicated newspaper column "In a Sow's Ear."

Gwen lives near Big Timber, Montana, where she raises miniature horses and works on her attitude.

DATE DUE